Oracle CX Cloud Suite

Deliver a seamless and personalized customer experience
with the Oracle CX Suite

Kresimir Juric

BIRMINGHAM - MUMBAI

Oracle CX Cloud Suite

Commissioning Editor: Richa Tripathi
Acquisition Editor: Sandeep Mishra
Content Development Editor: Tiksha Sarang
Technical Editor: Riddesh Dawne
Copy Editor: Safis Editing
Project Coordinator: Prajakta Naik
Proofreader: Safis Editing
Indexer: Pratik Shirodkar
Graphics: Jisha Chirayil
Production Coordinator: Jayalaxmi Raja

First published: March 2019

Production reference: 1290319

Published by Packt Publishing Ltd.
Livery Place
35 Livery Street
Birmingham
B3 2PB, UK.

ISBN 978-1-78883-493-3

www.packtpub.com

I would like to thank my loving and patient wife, Marijana, for her support, patience, and encouragement throughout the long process of writing this book.

- Kresimir Juric

`mapt.io`

Mapt is an online digital library that gives you full access to over 5,000 books and videos, as well as industry leading tools to help you plan your personal development and advance your career. For more information, please visit our website.

Why subscribe?

- Spend less time learning and more time coding with practical eBooks and Videos from over 4,000 industry professionals

- Improve your learning with Skill Plans built especially for you

- Get a free eBook or video every month

- Mapt is fully searchable

- Copy and paste, print, and bookmark content

Packt.com

Did you know that Packt offers eBook versions of every book published, with PDF and ePub files available? You can upgrade to the eBook version at `www.packt.com` and as a print book customer, you are entitled to a discount on the eBook copy. Get in touch with us at `customercare@packtpub.com` for more details.

At `www.packt.com`, you can also read a collection of free technical articles, sign up for a range of free newsletters, and receive exclusive discounts and offers on Packt books and eBooks.

Contributors

About the author

Kresimir Juric has spent many years in different positions and working with many different projects/clients. He has broad competence in designing and deploying various CX/CRM systems, helping customers grow their businesses and achieve their goals.

Kresimir has experience of introducing organizational change as an internal resource and as a consultant in organizations ranging from SOHO/SME to some of the biggest international corporations.

Kresimir has implemented CRM systems and organizational changes in the telecommunications, banking, hospitality, credit information, manufacturing, and pharmaceutical industries with the least possible organizational resistance.

About the reviewer

Hung Huynh graduated from University of Oslo with a master's degree.

He started his career as a system developer, creating IT tools to aid the construction of residential buildings. He later moved to Oracle and started a long career with Service-Oriented Architecture (SOA). He used his deep knowledge of the whole Oracle Fusion Middleware stack to help many customers to achieve their visions.

At the time of writing this, Hung Huynh has moved to the energy sector. Hung Huynh has held key positions such as architect and project manager for Sysco Digital Utility Platform.

Hung Huynh is an advocate for the data-driven approach to IT solutions. He has translated *The Dataleader's Manifesto* into both Norwegian and Vietnamese.

Packt is searching for authors like you

If you're interested in becoming an author for Packt, please visit `authors.packtpub.com` and apply today. We have worked with thousands of developers and tech professionals, just like you, to help them share their insight with the global tech community. You can make a general application, apply for a specific hot topic that we are recruiting an author for, or submit your own idea.

Table of Contents

Preface

With this book, we aim to familiarize the reader with all aspects of the Oracle **customer experience** (**CX**) and explain how to utilize these aspects to create the best customer experience possible.

This book will also teach the reader about the basics of business analysis, solution architecture, project management, and strategic thinking.

Finally, this book will use examples that combine everything that's learned in this book in the form of a use case scenario.

Who this book is for

This book is for everyone who has any interest in learning about Oracle CX and customer experience in general. This book caters to the technical, management, and organizational aspects of customer experience adoption and implementation. Whether you are a technical or business person, this book will explain all aspects of Oracle CX so that, in the end, you will understand the whole CX story.

What this book covers

Chapter 1, *The King Is Dead, Long Live the King,* lays the foundation for the book, helping to define the differences between CRM and CX solutions and the purpose of a customer's journey.

Chapter 2, *Overview of Products,* provides a description of and explains the most common use cases for all the solutions in the Oracle CX portfolio.

Chapter 3, *CX Solution Architecture,* describes possible solution architectures using Oracle CX solutions.

Chapter 4, *As-Is and To-Be Analysis,* discusses methodologies and tools used to conduct appropriate As-Is business analysis, understand the findings, and develop appropriate To-Be plans.

Chapter 5, *Adopting a Strategy - Organizational Changes*, discusses the need for organizational changes and the strategy needed for implementation so that the company is able to provide the best possible customer experience.

Chapter 6, *Organizing and Conducting an Implementation Project*, discusses how to organize and conduct an Oracle CX implementation project.

Chapter 7, *Scenarios and Deployments*, provides a general explanation of cloud computing and deployment types, and explains how Oracle CX can be used in cloud and hybrid deployments. After this chapter, you should be able to select an appropriate deployment option.

Chapter 8, *Case Study - Oracle CX Cloud*, takes all of the topics discussed in the previous chapter in order to design an Oracle CX solution with appropriate implementation strategy for a telecommunications company.

To get the most out of this book

The reader should have a general knowledge of the technical and organizational aspects of CRM systems and customer relations. It would be beneficial to have some knowledge of marketing activities, organizational structures, and project implementation processes.

Download the example code files

You can download the example code files for this book from your account at www.packt.com. If you purchased this book elsewhere, you can visit www.packt.com/support and register to have the files emailed directly to you.

You can download the code files by following these steps:

1. Log in or register at www.packt.com.
2. Select the **SUPPORT** tab.
3. Click on **Code Downloads & Errata**.
4. Enter the name of the book in the **Search** box and follow the onscreen instructions.

Once the file is downloaded, please make sure that you unzip or extract the folder using the latest version of:

- WinRAR/7-Zip for Windows
- Zipeg/iZip/UnRarX for Mac
- 7-Zip/PeaZip for Linux

We also have other code bundles from our rich catalog of books and videos available at `https://github.com/PacktPublishing/`. Check them out!

Download the color images

We also provide a PDF file that has color images of the screenshots/diagrams used in this book. You can download it here: `https://www.packtpub.com/sites/default/files/downloads/9781788834933_ColorImages.pdf`.

Conventions used

There are a number of text conventions used throughout this book.

`CodeInText`: Indicates code words in text, database table names, folder names, filenames, file extensions, pathnames, dummy URLs, user input, and Twitter handles. Here is an example: "After that, we can just mark in Excel from `Complaint 1` to `595`."

Bold: Indicates a new term, an important word, or words that you see onscreen. For example, words in menus or dialog boxes appear in the text like this. Here is an example: "Select Pareto diagram in **INSERT** | **statistical** charts menu of Excel."

Warnings or important notes appear like this.

Tips and tricks appear like this.

Get in touch

Feedback from our readers is always welcome.

General feedback: If you have questions about any aspect of this book, mention the book title in the subject of your message and email us at customercare@packtpub.com.

Errata: Although we have taken every care to ensure the accuracy of our content, mistakes do happen. If you have found a mistake in this book, we would be grateful if you would report this to us. Please visit www.packt.com/submit-errata, selecting your book, clicking on the Errata Submission Form link, and entering the details.

Piracy: If you come across any illegal copies of our works in any form on the Internet, we would be grateful if you would provide us with the location address or website name. Please contact us at copyright@packt.com with a link to the material.

If you are interested in becoming an author: If there is a topic that you have expertise in and you are interested in either writing or contributing to a book, please visit authors.packtpub.com.

Reviews

Please leave a review. Once you have read and used this book, why not leave a review on the site that you purchased it from? Potential readers can then see and use your unbiased opinion to make purchase decisions, we at Packt can understand what you think about our products, and our authors can see your feedback on their book. Thank you!

For more information about Packt, please visit packt.com.

Section 1: Brave New World

In this section, we will go through the various concepts
of **customer relationship management** (**CRM**) and customer experience and understand
the differences between them, explore what each Oracle CX suite offers, and finally look
into Oracle solutions and **Single Sign-On** (**SSO**).

The following chapters will be covered in this section:

- Chapter 1, *The King Is Dead, Long Live the King*
- Chapter 2, *Overview of Products*
- Chapter 3, *CX Solution Architecture*

The King Is Dead, Long Live the King

1

You must be familiar with the term **customer relationship management** (**CRM**). Companies have adopted CRM to the degree that even technical and business departments are called CRM, or have CRM as a part of their name.

In this chapter, we will compare CRM and **customer experience** (**CX**) and explain the differences.

You will learn about the following topics:

- CRM and its shortcomings
- The customer journey of CX and the need for it
- How CX enables us to accomplish objectives for the best customer experience

Learning about CRM

Like many other contemporary concepts, the concept of CRM in everyday practice provokes doubts related to its meaning and its scope. The reason for this lies in the fact that CRM is both a strategy, a process, and a system. It is difficult to define a concept that is ambiguous because it covers such a wide area. It should be noted that CRM is a concept developed within the framework of marketing relations and business philosophy that strives to meet the individual needs of consumers; making consumers happy and building systematic interaction with consumers transforms them into clients. In order to do this, a communication system needs to be established that will ensure immediate interaction with the consumer.

Through such interaction, anonymous individuals as mass consumers are transformed into individualized and personalized units, which not only systematically collect information, but also systematically provide information. That in itself presents a challenge when discussing CRM, since strategy, processes, and systems are part of one whole system. We will focus on all of these areas in this book, but for this chapter, we will mainly focus on the systems aspect of CRM.

Such a communication system, especially in the case of a large number of consumers, cannot be built without the use of modern technology. That's why CRM systems integrate into marketing and information systems, as well as management systems. Data is the basis for creating a consumer image and consumer profile that contains all the information and connections that you deem relevant; that is, a 360-degree view of the consumer, which effectively enables you to cater to their needs. Such a system also enables the selection of quality clients in terms of securing loyal consumers. Consequently, CRM enables the construction of a defensive marketing strategy that seeks to retain consumers and make good use of existing clients, which, in nature, requires less effort and resources than the implementation of an offensive marketing strategy.

CRM covers a complete sales process, and its strength manifests from contact between businesses and individual consumers. CRM has a presence not only in area sales activities, but is important in pre-sale and post-sale activities. CRM has evolved from so-called **call centers** that, except for sales purposes, and were used for post-sale activities, for supporting users of products or services.

CRM is currently a key component of ensuring modern businesses survive.

The benefits of CRM

CRM software is used for customer-information systems and capturing, storing, processing, and sharing data within a company.

The main benefits of this are as follows:

- The IT system organizations need to support CRM systems which enforce you to define the roles of surrounding systems and to integrate them accordingly
- Data is kept in a highly organized and accessible manner, and CRM usually comes with predefined dataset relationships
- Data security
- A uniformed consumer view, that is, a 360-degree view
- A product and services catalogue

- **Configure, Price, and Quote** (CPQ) functionalities
- Data analytics with drill-down reports
- Process engines
- Business rules engines
- Campaign management
- Loyalty management
- A sales funnel and pipeline
- Customizable user interfaces
- Case management

These benefits are organizational, providing a great inside view of your organization, which enables you to optimize your internal processes and resource usage, while preventing errors using the business rules and process engines.

The limitations of CRM

CRM imposes significant limitations on organizations that implement it. These limitations were not apparent for 20 years, but now they are hindering businesses in their efforts to deliver a great customer experience, and impose technical complications with exorbitant financial costs.

The most common problems with implementing CRM are those that stem from an organization's inconsistencies. Simply put, they occur when CRM is run by a separate department or departments within an organization, and there is no real perception of a CRM end-to-end strategy. These departments are most often marketing departments, specialized CRM departments, or sales departments. Relationships with consumers are not painful in the aforementioned departments; problems usually arise in departments that are in contact with consumers, such as customer service, personnel in stores, and so on. These departments usually do not have enough influence when the time comes to define CRM solutions, strategies, and processes. Relationships with users are not painful in parts of the organization that are, by their nature, tuned to their needs; problems arise elsewhere.

Contemporary organizations usually have obscure units, such as police cells, whose task is to sanction *naughty* users. Sadly, such departments often use traditional police methods from the era of an economic system that was common to the whole world, regardless of the political system. It is a kind of economic communism, or a monopoly. One bidding, one showing attitude toward users, which in essence comes down to the phrase *you need us and we know what is best for you*, or, as Ford said, *you can get model T in any color you want, as long it is black*. With fierce competition today, this approach is not a viable business strategy.

CRM systems fails to incorporate customer experience and customer needs in all departments, including departments that are, by nature, not customer-facing. To enable an appropriate customer experience, applications and strategies must be accepted by the whole organization in an easy and encompassing manner.

Organizational limitations

Although CRM usually involves a substantial amount of information regarding customers, data is used only for maximizing profit and does not take into account what is important to the customer. This kind of thinking is called **inside-out thinking**.

Inside-out thinking

The features of inside-out thinking include the following:

- A company is concerned only about the baseline
- Appropriate customer experience is not imperative
- More importance is given to internal processes than to processes that tailor interactions with customers or partners
- Budgets are always assigned to internal needs
- Usually, an incorrect process triggers the implementation of inappropriate systems and, subsequently, assigning people to roles whose incompetent or are inappropriate

Technical limitations

CRM is a monolithic system, and the purchase of your CRM will enable you to cover some parts of your customer-relationship strategy, but not all, and not in a good manner.

Integrating CRM with other applications and systems is not an easy task, and there are many caveats to consider and compromises to be made.

Time to market (**TTM**) can be long, which makes it costly. Usually, any change in CRM triggers changes in a myriad of other systems.

Reasons for leaving CRM in the past

It is no secret that the majority of CRM-implementation projects fail or do not deliver appropriate value to a company. The usual method for CRM adoption is *Big Bang*, which demonstrates that most organizations still consider CRM, and subsequently, customer interaction, in a very rigid manner. With this method of implementation, there is very little space left for adopting changes that are needed to respond to the ever-changing business environment and consumer needs. It is not enough to implement CRM on time and inside budget. Technology needs to be flexible so that companies can rapidly incorporate new strategies and business objectives during the implementation of CRM. In a sense, CX/CRM projects do not end; they need to evolve alongside the market's evolution.

A CRM system, as a monolithic system, is not able to be flexible, no matter how well you have planned it or how skilled your team is. Another important aspect is that CRM systems are not tailored to support new channels of communication, such as cell phones and social media channels. CRM systems are great as a transactional database, and that was good enough for 20 years, but in today's world they are holding businesses back.

The customer experience of CX

CRM systems are great for storing and managing customer-related information. However, CRM systems fail to tailor communication, and, subsequently, the experience that customers have with companies, catering predominantly to organizational, internal needs.

Customer experience implies a holistic approach and this includes all the times a customer is in touch with the company or brand (that is, via the web and advertising, considering a factors such as reputation, packaging, location, delivery speed, ease of use, reliability, and so on); this is appropriate customer care.

Every client's experience with an organization provokes an emotional response. This could be a pleasant experience if they encounter good things when interacting with a business or they could have a bad experience. The experience of a transaction with an organization, that is, how well a client is treated, remains with the buyer, and affects their future decisions.

If you do not provide a personal touch and do not behave toward the client as an individual, then you are showing that you do not acknowledge their needs in an appropriate manner, and so you do not really care about them.

A CX system defines customer loyalty as the emotional connection that clients have with the organization. Customer engagement describes the health of the relationship between the buyer and the brand. It defines it as how well an organization delivers what it has promised through its brand, to what extent it has a fair relationship with its customers, and how well it deals with complaints and objections.

As part of the complaint process, a company must first develop an understanding that, a client who has had a good experience becomes an organization's or brand's promoter, and transmits that information through word of mouth, thus becoming an ambassador for the brand. Have you thought about rewarding those who complain? We are asking the question, *how do you provide a good service?*

Each time a customer complains, the damage to the customer is twofold—the economic cost of making the complaint and the emotional damage. Companies that do not recognize the emotional damage caused by customer complaints fail to enable their employees to recognize it too, risking the most important thing, and that is loyalty:

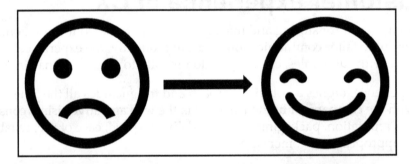

CX is not about data management, it is not about internal systems; its main goal is to make the experience simple and transparent for the customer.

The objectives of the technology are as follows:

- To create a single, integrated, engaging, and highly personalized customer experience
- To create omnichannel communication, seamlessly integrated into one screen
- To create a unified platform that provides social, predictive analytics, and enables integration with other systems

Organizational benefits

CX technology enables businesses to tailor customer experiences and use data in the best time and way to create the best possible customer experience, essentially allowing companies to think in an outside-in manner.

A customer-centric philosophy

For the successful introduction of a CX system, a vision is needed that will encompass the entire business, and must start at the highest organizational level. A customer-centric philosophy takes into account the financial objectives and business strategy of the company, and upgrades the marketing strategy. It determines how the company builds profitable relationships with clients and gains their trust.

The introduction of CX technology is not enough by itself; it is necessary to change the culture, organizational structure, and priorities of the company.

This, in a nutshell, describes a company with a customer-centric philosophy.

Outside-in thinking

The features of outside-in thinking include the following:

- Understanding customer needs and objectives
- Listening to your customers and taking note of what they need and suggest
- Always thinking about how your decisions impact your customers
- Making the experience easier and more transparent for your customers
- Using the customer-journey technique to map exercises frequently
- Closing the loop using customer feedback

The technological benefits of CX

CX suite is not a monolithic system like CRM systems are, which, in itself, is a substantial benefit. CX enables businesses to tailor the system to their needs, to quickly change systems, and to adopt a new strategy when needed, all while offering a great customer experience.

Data integration between systems is seamless and data is kept in an appropriate system. It has much easier implementation; since you do not have to implement a large monolithic system, and there is no need for the big bang approach.

The key capabilities of CX

Nowadays, a sustainable competitive advantage can be best achieved if value proposition is really needed for users—save time for your customers by quickly and easily finding out why this product or service will be bought by consumers. After this process, customers will have growing confidence in your company, because you are speaking truthfully about the advantages and disadvantages of your products and services in a simple way.

The customer knows exactly what is waiting for them in the buying process, and knows how, after the purchase, they will contact you if there is a problem or they have an additional desire. When these qualities are transmitted to the online environment in the context of easily finding what they are looking for, the key to success is to create comprehensible content for users and a customized user experience for prospective clients. Various studies have shown that customer experience will be the most important segment of organizational advancement in the coming years.

Optimizing user experience has the goal of simplifying and speeding up processes, and enabling the easy completion of the requested action.

Oracle CX is a set of applications that form a strategic end-to-end platform for companies. Oracle CX is enabling companies to implement and maintain CX capabilities in their business. These applications are shown in the following diagram:

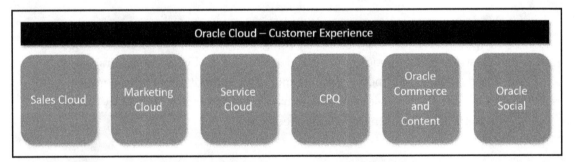

The Oracle CX cloud consists of the following applications:

- The Oracle **Sales Cloud** provides tools for customer data management, sales cataloging, sales force automation, sales prediction, analytics, and communication with customers and partners.
- The **Marketing Cloud** is used for creating campaigns and tracking them throughout their lifespan. Campaigns can be personalized for each customer or segment. Customers can be segmented using all the information available from the Marketing Cloud or another application that you are using in your company.

- The **Service Cloud** is used for customer service management. This application is mainly used in contact centers and enables companies to track customer cases using its omnichannel-communication capabilities.
- The **CPQ** application enables users to establish pricing and quoting processes so that they can easily manage and update product pricing and orders.
- The **Oracle Commerce and Content** applications use templates and other pre-built components, enabling users to implement and manage their storefronts on the web.
- The **Oracle Social** application combines **latent semantic analysis** (**LSA**), **natural language processing** (**NLP**), and its own proprietary algorithms to provide comprehensive social listening, analysis, and social engagement features.

Summary

In this chapter, we have covered topics describing the differences between CRM and CX. We have explained why companies need to adopt a CX implementation approach, and we have described a CX portfolio.

The sunset of current technological and social CRM developments shows that it is high time for companies to have systems that are able to translate the benefits of products/services into a language that is comprehensible to users, and to adapt the way they present their products/services to users.

There are four essential principles of customer experience:

- Interaction must be in both directions customer-company and company-customer, and the loop must be closed.
- The customer must be engaged in every step of communication.
- The company has to be able to cater to the customer's needs and wants.
- The customer must be able to choose. This shows that the company values them and tailors the experience specially for them. The selection process must be easy and transparent for customers to understand and use.

That is customer experience in a nutshell.

In the next chapter, we will see how it can be implemented in the real world using Oracle's CX offering. We will also discuss best practices and prerequisites.

Overview of Products

2

People today have interaction with multiple sales channels, with multiple devices, and share experiences using social media. Recognizing the impact of today's possibilities is essential for sustaining and growing an enterprise's business. To help your business thrive in today's sales environment, Oracle offers a whole suite of solutions—Oracle CX.

In this chapter, we will explain the main topics covered in this book, focusing on business benefits. The goal of this chapter is to ensure that you understand the role of each of these solutions.

Here is what we will cover in this chapter:

- Oracle Sales Cloud
- Oracle Marketing Cloud
- Oracle Service Cloud
- Oracle CPQ Cloud
- Oracle Commerce
- Oracle Social Cloud
- Oracle CX

Oracle solutions and their roles in an enterprise

We will now explain in which cases you should use Oracle Cloud solutions; we will not go into the solutions themselves and how to use them.

Before you read on, you should be familiar with the principle of **Master Data Management (MDM)**.

MDM is a method that helps you to define the flow of data in your organization while maintaining data integrity and a single point of reference.

Essentially, what it means is that you should keep data as a contact address in one system; other systems should only retrieve it when needed, keep it for processing, and delete it after processing is finished and not store it. Other systems should not permanently store data for which they are not the MDM system.

Oracle Sales Cloud

Oracle Sales Cloud is the closest you can come to a traditional **Customer Relationship Management (CRM)** solution. Like all other CX solutions in the CX suite, it can be used in isolation or combined with other offerings.

Oracle Sales Cloud's primary role in a complex deployment should be giving a 360-degree view of your contacts and customers; that is, Oracle Sales Cloud should be the MDM system for contacts and customers.

In CRM terminology, a **contact** is a person and an **account** is a company.

In the example of John Smith, CEO of ACME inc., the contact/account designation would be as follows:

- **Contact**: John Smith
- **Account**: ACME inc.

Oracle Sales Cloud to other systems

Other systems in your enterprise architecture should not keep this information; they should be integrated with Oracle Sales Cloud and use views, queries, or API calls to get this information when needed.

Other systems to Oracle Sales Cloud

Other systems, such as Marketing Cloud, Service Cloud, and CPQ, should be used to enrich the 360 view in your Sales Cloud solution, providing information through views, queries, or APIs.

The following are some examples of data used to enrich the 360-degree view:

- Promotions history
- Cases raised and their status
- Goods purchased
- Content browsed on your page

Oracle Marketing Cloud

Oracle Marketing Cloud shines when used with other solutions, such as Social Cloud and Sales Cloud.

A typical role for Oracle Marketing Cloud would be managing your campaigns and segmenting your contacts and customers.

As we mentioned in the description of Oracle Sales Cloud, data about your contacts and customers should be imported for campaign and segmentation purposes, and not maintained in Oracle Marketing Cloud.

Other systems to Oracle Marketing Cloud

Oracle Marketing Cloud should receive data needed for segmentation or campaigns from other systems.

For example, information that should be received in Oracle Marketing Cloud could include the following:

- Names
- Surnames
- Email addresses
- Phone numbers
- Addresses
- Total consumption
- Number of cases with positive resolution
- Number of cases with negative resolution

This information should be retrieved with views, queries, or API calls from other systems.

For example, if you are a telecommunications company, you could use this information to segment your contacts according to cases and consumption to give them promotions if they had an interruption in service.

Oracle Marketing Cloud to other systems

Since Marketing Cloud can track responses to campaigns and segment your contacts and customers according to logic that you have defined, you could use that information to enrich your 360 views.

For example, you could use this kind of logic:

- Has answered to the last three campaigns
- Is segmented as gold
- Is segmented as silver
- Is segmented as bronze

This information should not be maintained in other systems; it should be delivered using views, queries, or API calls.

Oracle Service Cloud

Oracle Service Cloud is a solution that can be used in your contact center. If your service cloud receives a call, your staff will be able to see all cases about that contact or customer, leveraging the customer-contact relationship details found in Oracle Sales Cloud.

The solution supports multiple-channel communication and can be integrated with telephony solutions so that your support staff can communicate through all channels at any time.

Another use of Oracle Service Cloud would be to lower the number of calls or emails your back office receives, lowering the **Average Handle Time** (**AHT**) and load on teams through integrated knowledge and smart assistant features.

For team leaders, Oracle Service Cloud provides analytics so that you can have weekly, monthly, yearly, or adhoc reports.

Other systems to Oracle Service Cloud

Information that is beneficial to Oracle Service Cloud includes the following:

- Contact-customer relationship details
- Email addresses
- Addresses
- Campaign response details
- Purchases

This information should not be maintained in Oracle Service Cloud; it should be retrieved using views, queries, or API calls.

Oracle Service Cloud to other systems

Since Oracle Service Cloud is usually a system to be used in your contact center, it should be a system through which updates to other systems are done.

The following are examples of data that should be sent from Oracle Service Cloud:

- Contact information updates
- Cases
- Incidents

This information should not be maintained in other systems; it should be delivered using views, queries, or API calls.

Oracle CPQ Cloud

CPQ in **Oracle CPQ Cloud** stands for **Configure**, **Price**, and **Quote**. Essentially, you would like to keep your product catalog in this solution. Another important functionality that is provided in Oracle CPQ Cloud is the ability to specify price lists per country, per company, or per segment.

Oracle CPQ Cloud is a solution through which your sales force will send quotes to your customers.

Other systems to Oracle CPQ Cloud

Since we have mentioned that you can design specific price lists for products in Oracle CPQ Cloud, information that can help you from other systems could include the following:

- Age
- Address
- Segmentation

This information should not be maintained in Oracle CPQ Cloud; it should be retrieved using views, queries, or API calls.

Oracle CPQ Cloud to other systems

Oracle CPQ Cloud holds your product catalog, and as such it can provide other systems with product and purchase data. With this in mind, information provided to other systems could include the following:

- Information about products
- Quotes
- Purchases
- The salesperson connected to the quote or sale

This information should not be maintained in other systems; it should be delivered using views, queries, or API calls.

Oracle Commerce Cloud

Oracle Commerce Cloud can be used to design your pages and web stores, as well as to easily maintain them and change them to respond to market needs in an agile manner. The site is optimized for mobile devices and computer screens.

Another significant feature of these solutions is B2B capabilities, which enable your company's B2B collaborations.

Other systems to Oracle Commerce Cloud

Data that can be sent from other systems to Oracle Commerce Cloud includes customer information and product information, such as the following:

- Customer information
- Product information
- Pricing lists
- Customer ID
- Loyalty points
- Campaign information

With this information, you are able to personalize the experience of your sites to suit the needs of your customers.

This information should not be maintained in Oracle Service Cloud; it should be retrieved using views, queries, or API calls.

Oracle Commerce Cloud to other systems

Oracle Commerce and Oracle Content Cloud can provide significant insight about your customers, which can be used in Oracle Marketing and Oracle CPQ Cloud. You can also allow customers to change their data in Sales Cloud through these solutions.

An example of data that can be sent from Oracle Commerce and Oracle Content Cloud is as follows:

- Which sites customers have opened
- Where on the site customers are positioning their cursors
- How many times a customer looked at some promotion

Data can be used for personalized campaigns in which you target the exact products in which your customer is showing interest.

This information should not be maintained in other systems; it should be delivered using views, queries, or API calls.

Oracle Social Cloud

Oracle Social Cloud is both an internal- and external-facing solution. It can be used to provide your internal resources with a social platform and facilitate the flow of ideas in your company and/or enable your company to engage with and listen to your customers.

All of your internal teams, from marketing to HR, can understand the sentiment of social networks and communicate in an appropriate manner.

Other systems to Oracle Social Cloud

You can use Oracle Social Cloud to drive personalized campaigns, address incidents, or communicate with possible hires using social networks.

Data that could be used by Oracle Social Cloud includes the following:

- Campaign data
- Contact information
- Case information
- HR announcements

This information should not be maintained in Oracle Social Cloud; it should be retrieved using views, queries, or API calls.

Oracle Social Cloud to other systems

Social Cloud can be used as an input system for other solutions in Oracle CX, offering functionality to do with sentiment, per-case communication with customers, campaign responses, and more.

Here are some examples of data that can be sent to other systems from Social Cloud:

- Campaign sentiment
- Campaign responses
- Case responses

This information should not be maintained in other systems; it should be delivered using views, queries, or API calls.

Oracle Sales Cloud resembling a CRM

Oracle Sales Cloud is the Oracle offering that most closely resembles a CRM. It can be used as a standalone solution and can do all tasks reasonably well, but the real power of the Oracle CX suite is unlocked if it is paired with other solutions.

Oracle Sales Cloud is available anywhere, anytime, and on any device, whether it's your desktop, smartphone, or tablet. You can use it through a browser interface or by using an app on your mobile phone or tablet.

An extremely useful feature of the Oracle Sales Cloud application is that it can be used offline, so there is no situation in which your sales force will not be able to negotiate and close deals. The application provides sales intelligence through reports and dashboards. The application provides you with key insights so that you can make informed decisions—anytime, anywhere.

The application can also support your decision making using a built-in forecasting feature, which enables your sales force to focus on good opportunities and prioritize their efforts.

If you need to show results or make an interface for your superiors so that they are always aware of processes, Oracle Sales Cloud comes with six pre-built, interactive visual reports.

Using the App Designer tool, you can make your own dashboards to cater to your needs.

For the purpose of managing your sales efforts, Oracle Sales Cloud comes with unit modeling functionalities. Unit modeling enables you to outline territories and assign opportunities, and leads to specific business units.

Here are the main features of Oracle Sales Cloud:

- 360 view
- Sales catalog
- Social network
- Sales Cloud on smartphones and tablets
- Sales Cloud Salesforce automation
- Sales Cloud Analytics
- Sales Cloud Sales predictor
- Sales Cloud for Outlook
- Sales Cloud for IBM Notes
- Sales Cloud Sales Performance Management
- Sales Cloud Partner Relationship Management

- Sales Cloud configuration, customization, and integrations
- Sales Cloud for Communications
- Sales Cloud for Consumer Goods
- Sales Cloud for Financial Services
- Oracle Enterprise Contracts
- Sales Cloud for high tech and manufacturing
- Sales Cloud Migration Utility for Oracle CRM on demand
- Oracle Incentive Compensation
- Oracle Sales Cloud Territory Management
- Sales forecasting
- Sales campaigns

As is evident, Oracle Sales Cloud comes packed with functionalities, with both horizontal and vertical solutions. Covering them all would take a book on its own.

Customer data management

One of the most important tasks of any CRM system is customer data management, and Oracle Sales Cloud is the repository of your all data, so its task is to keep customer data neat and organized no matter what changes you introduce.

Consistent data is of the utmost significance to any organization. Oracle Sales Cloud customer data management helps you to consolidate account and contact data from multiple sources, standardize fields, and resolve duplicate conflicts, which enables you to have an appropriate customer profile.

Oracle is known for being the best database company, and the excellence and knowledge that was used to create Oracle DB is present in Oracle Sales Cloud. That does not mean you should understand how databases work or what PL/SQL is. Oracle Sales Cloud enables you to design and maintain your customer data.

Oracle Sales Cloud is built upon source hierarchy and cross-referencing components. What does that mean? When you have an already defined account, contact entities and the established connections between them are very important. So, consider an example of a person John Smith and company ACME inc., a relationship that John Smith (a CEO) has with an employee of ACME inc. is an out-of-the-box feature; there is no need for you to define it.

If you need a special type of object that does not come with Oracle Sales Cloud, you can define it yourself.

This solves major challenges and problems connected to the maintenance and cleanup of customer data.

In the end, it all boils down to you having the appropriate information when you need it.

Integrations

Now that we have covered data design and maintenance, the next question is, *How can I leverage my data?*

Luckily, Oracle Sales Cloud comes equipped with purpose-built functionalities so that you can address this question in the best manner.

You can use the integration app or you can use a REST API to develop your own integrations.

Just as all roads lead to Rome, all data leads to Oracle Sales Cloud.

Conclusion

Oracle CX Cloud is the heart of your customer data, so be sure that you design your data accordingly and maintain it vigilantly, since any error in Oracle Sales Cloud will propagate to all other integrated systems.

Oracle Marketing Cloud

Oracle Marketing is not a standalone product, but a suite of marketing tools.

These are the marketing tools in Oracle Marketing Cloud:

- Oracle Eloqua
- Oracle Responsys
- Oracle BlueKai
- Oracle Maxymiser
- Oracle Infinity
- Content Marketing
- Social Marketing

These solutions answer the million-dollar question: how can you utilize innovation to cater to your customers' needs?

Oracle Eloqua

Oracle Eloqua is used for marketing automation, that is, for the creation of personalized campaigns across multiple channels.

Oracle Eloqua comes with the support of 500 partners comprising 700 integrations, all of which can be used in your campaigns.

The main features are as follows:

- Targeting and segmentation
- Campaign management
- Lead management
- Marketing measurement
- Sales and marketing alignment

These features enable you to do the following:

- Personalize campaigns
- Understand customer sentiment
- Get real-time customer feedback and insight regarding your campaigns
- Enrich account and contact data
- Unite campaign data from multiple channels
- Create refined customer segmentations
- Graphically design and understand campaigns
- Easily deploy adaptive campaigns
- Enrich lead data with multiple models on a single contact
- Use closed-loop reporting to track the success of your campaigns and act accordingly
- Use web analytics to see who is visiting your pages and why
- Get a complete customer activity picture in your campaigns, including web activity, emails opened, form submits, and social activity

Oracle Responsys

Oracle Responsys is used to manage and orchestrate marketing interactions with customers across email, mobile, social media, display, and the web.

The main features of Oracle Responsys are as follows:

- Email marketing
- Program orchestration
- Email campaign testing
- Mobile marketing
- Analytics and insights
- Commerce marketing

These features enable you to do the following:

- Personalize email communication
- Coordinate email marketing
- Reduce messaging fragmentation
- Get message previews on multiple devices
- Create consumer paths
- Create a customer journey and avoid the journey to nowhere
- Increase customer lifetime value
- Easily test email campaigns manually or automatically
- Integrated testing, provides near real-time test results enabling you faster deployment
- Use push, rich push, in-app, SMS, and MMS messaging
- Analytics

Oracle BlueKai

Oracle BlueKai is used for marketing data management. It enables you to understand the data that you have gathered in your campaigns. Essentially, it is a cloud-based big data platform.

BlueKai currently has over 300 partners, in categories such as media, search, email, and analytics.

The main features are as follows:

- Cross-device support
- ID graph
- Media and data ecosystem

These features enable you to do the following:

- Visualize and plan campaigns across devices using the audience builder tool
- Analyze data across devices using the device ID
- Match devices to customers
- Do inventory counts against first- and third-party data
- Onboard offline data using an ID graph
- Enrich first-party data
- Accurately identify customers across devices
- Share data easily with other solutions

Oracle Maxymiser

Oracle Maxymiser is used for the testing and optimization of your campaigns, web, mobile pages, and apps.

For example, it can give you answers to questions such as these:

- How does my test scenario impact long-term retention?
- Do tested users convert faster than others?
- What are the unforeseen consequences of my test scenarios?

With Oracle Maxymiser, you can prevent bad campaigns from happening or you can explore new, never-before-imagined opportunities.

Its features enable you to do the following:

- Personalize your B2B and B2C customer experience
- Discover missed opportunities
- Run complex tests easily
- Make accurate, data-driven decisions
- Perform server-side web optimization
- Optimize your site for any screen

Oracle Infinity

Oracle Infinity is used for marketing data analytics. It is an analytics platform used for tracking, measuring, and optimizing visitor behavior on your sites and apps.

The main features are as follows:

- Data collection
- Reports
- Streams
- Action center
- Integrations
- Roles
- Library

These features enable you to do the following:

- Precisely collect web and mobile data
- Evaluate and augment data
- Analyze data through the UI or using APIs
- Use reports
- Use streams to gain insights into the flow of visitor data
- Integrate systems such as CRMs in your sessions
- Use the integration API to integrate with other systems
- Manage role, group, and privilege definitions
- Manage reports, measures, dimensions, segments, or any other object

Oracle Content Marketing

Oracle Content Marketing is used to create digital presence that can be used in your campaigns or in any stage of the sales cycle. It enables you to create relevant communications that lead to conversion.

The main features are as follows:

- Planning content
- Collaboration and workflows
- Content distribution
- Content analytics

These features enable you to do the following:

- Gain a unified view of activities
- Get visual representations of activities
- Drill down to get more information
- Set workflow definitions and assignments based on author, category, project, or content type
- Use content guides and content scoring to optimize terms with suggestions and best practices
- Translate content with **Language Service Providers** (**LSPs**)
- Enable sales to quickly find and share relevant content
- Publish on a defined scale while ensuring compliance and branding
- Achieve granularity such that each team can manage its own content
- Track engagement
- See content impact by a person
- Modify and test content to see the audience response

Social Marketing

Social Marketing enables you to listen to social conversations, publish relevant content, engage with customers, and analyze social data.

Social Marketing uses **Latent Semantic Analysis** (**LSA**), which enables you to understand the sentiment of your customers.

The main features are as follows:

- Social listening
- Social analytics
- Social publishing and engagement

These features enable you to do the following:

- Remove irrelevant results using LSA
- Refine searches using filtering options
- Access over 40 million social sites
- Evaluate likes, actions, and shares
- Add social tags to your campaigns

- Use actionable recommendations to more effectively engage with your customers
- View all activities across all social channels
- Configure content streams
- Use the social inbox to respond to all messages across all channels in a timely manner
- See what content engages customers the most

Conclusion

If you have a feeling that each of the Oracle Marketing Cloud solutions could be used as a standalone product, your hunch is right.

All of these products were acquired by Oracle, and each of them is best of breed, but when used together and with roles assigned correctly, they become much more than the sum of their parts.

Oracle Service Cloud

Oracle Service Cloud is another acquired offering. It was formerly known as **RightNow**.

RightNow was known as the best-of-breed contact center and customer service solution, and it continues to fulfill that role as Oracle's CX offering. Oracle Service Cloud encompasses everything that you need so that your contact center can provide the best possible experience to your customers.

The main components of Oracle Service Cloud are as follows:

- **Oracle RightNow Web Experience**: This is a self-service platform that enables your customers to manage their options, subscriptions, contact data, and to submit cases. What they can manage depends on your design. An example case would be to allow customers to change their subscription. The subscription should be stored in Oracle Sales Cloud, and, upon customers login, it should be acquired using an API call and presented to the customer alongside all subscriptions the customer can migrate to. The last step should be the customer verification of the change followed by the data changing in Oracle Sales Cloud through an API call.
- **RightNow Social Experience**: This is another part of Oracle CX suite that offers you the opportunity to manage your social interactions. Oracle CX Cloud enables you to share roles between different offerings to best suit your needs.

- **RightNow Contact Center Experience**: This functionality enables you to manage communication with customers through a unified interface. If paired with Oracle Field Service, it can help you to facilitate communication between your technician teams and customers.
- **RightNow Policy Automation**: This enables you to tailor your communication with your customers using channels that are at your disposal.
- **RightNow Engage**: This consists of marketing automation and analytics. Yet again, these features are accessible through other solutions; you can decide which of the offerings suits your needs best.

Since this is a solution for contact centers, there are a few kinds of agent desktops that you can use:

- **Standalone Chat Dynamic Agent Desktop**: This comes with Oracle App Builder, which enables you to customize your working environment to suit your needs. The chat functionality is not only limited to communication but can also be used to conduct surveys. To help you in your day-to-day tasks, it comes equipped with a knowledge base and contract management functionalities.
- **Standard Dynamic Agent Desktop**: The standard version expands functionalities significantly from the standalone version. It comes with the Agent Desktop application, opportunities tracking functionality, and a mobile app. With this version, you are able to track your incidents through all channels of communication that are at your customers' disposal.
- **Enterprise Dynamic Agent Desktop**: The enterprise version enhances functionalities further, with customer feedback functionality and social monitoring. The main advantage of this version is guided assistance, which enables customers to resolve issues on their own.
- **Enterprise Contact Center Dynamic Agent Desktop**: This version further includes automation functionalities using scripting and workflows. It enables you also to register products so that an agent in the contact center is able to provide appropriate assistance for a product connected to your customer.

The main features are as follows:

- Integrations, especially with telephony
- Self-service tools for customers
- APIs that support OpenAPI
- Cross-channel interaction with your customers

- Social listening with the intent/sentiment
- Automation tools
- Self-service tools for customers

These features enable you to do the following:

- Decrease AHT
- Enable customers to find answers themselves
- Provides your company with the ability to contact customers using any channel in any step of the communication
- Use the self-service portal to enable your customers to manage their own data and services
- Listen to social channels and build your workflows according to response or sentiment
- Create custom dashboards and reports per role
- Have a view of each individual customer and all related communications
- Use the knowledge base with semantic searches
- Automate campaigns through any channel

Conclusion

Oracle Service Cloud provides you with a unified interface that enables you to monitor and engage with customers over any channel that is available to you. Since it is a part of the Oracle CX suite, it enables you to easily integrate with other offerings and unlock the full potential of your CX environment.

Oracle CPQ Cloud

CPQ is a process within the sales life cycle. Each business that sells a complicated product incorporates a CPQ method in some way or another. Once a client is curious about a product, the salesperson should put together the quote to satisfy the customer's request.

If a business sells a straightforward product with set costs, the CPQ method is already done; however, enterprise businesses usually have thousands of complicated products, changing rating calculations, massive proposal document templates, and sales that don't give enough time to address CPQ appropriately.

The main features of Oracle CPQ Cloud are listed here:

- Product configuration
- Guided selling
- Rule-driven search
- Pricing
- Discounting
- Approval workflows
- Proposal management
- eSignature
- Order execution

These features enable you to do the following:

- Configure and maintain complex products and services
- Cross-sell and up-sell
- Use region-based offerings
- Manage complex pricing based on the myriad of customer, regional, or time-based data
- Implement dynamic promotions based on customer, volume, regional, or time-based data
- Have approvals managed by workflows in order to streamline processes
- Use templates and easily create proposals
- Use out-of-the-box ERP integrations that enable fast order execution

Conclusion

The process has seen many changes in recent years. Oracle CPQ Cloud enables you to optimize flow, speed, accuracy, and efficiency throughout all areas of your business.

Usually, CPQ software is considered to be a necessity for large, enterprise-sized businesses, but Oracle also offers CPQ Cloud for mid-sized companies.

Oracle Commerce Cloud

Oracle Commerce Cloud has two main parts for two main use cases: Oracle Commerce for Retail and Oracle Commerce for B2B.

Oracle Commerce for Retail is used for B2C transactions, such as selling products and services to consumers.

Oracle Commerce for B2B, as the name implies, is used for B2B transactions, such as selling products and services to other companies.

The main features are as follows:

- Unified admin
- Platform and APIs
- Responsive storefront
- Guided search
- SEO
- Experience creation
- Loyalty framework
- Content management
- Catalog management
- Promotions
- Multisite management
- Personalization
- Product recommendations
- Transactional emails
- Social wish list and plugins
- B2B and B2C model payments
- Tax agent console
- Assisted selling application
- Adaptive intelligence security
- Integrations

These features enable you to do the following:

- Achieve an optimized UI using drag and drop tools
- Manage site experience
- Use Developer Studio to manage configurations so that the user experience is unified across all devices
- Have simple integrations using APIs
- Use Storefront, which comes with 35 languages and 60 currencies out of the box and can be easily customized and expended to suit your brand's needs

- Use guided search, which enables you to manage and scale search of your store
- Use SEO features to easily optimize for SEO gains using a myriad of in-built functionalities
- Manage your catalog easily, with functionalities to do with products, pricing, and inventory
- Manage B2B customer-specific settings
- Easily manage promotions
- Manage experience based on consumer or customer lifetime, average order value, last purchase amount, number of orders, registration date, first purchase date, last visit date, and more
- Implement experimental and scenario testing for flawless deployments
- Boost engagement with the loyalty framework
- Create non-catalog pages
- Send emails based on site-related activities
- Use social plugins to share your messages and wish lists on social networks
- Use payment gateways by only entering your credentials
- Use one platform to unify your B2B and B2C activities
- Use machine learning and AI to manage your engagement
- Use integrated reports

Conclusion

Oracle Commerce Cloud is an extensive and unified solution for B2B and B2C companies. It has a myriad of advanced features, and when paired with other solutions in Oracle CX, it can contribute well to the overall architecture of your storefront.

Oracle Social

Social media is to do with much more than marketing; it's about what directly influences purchases and customer loyalty. Oracle Social Cloud addresses this part of your business by helping you to nurture existing relationships, gain new customers, and even recruit the best talent.

Oracle Social Cloud is not meant to be used only as an external-facing solution; it should also be used by your internal teams to enable seamless communication. For example, HR teams may use it to contact possible recruits.

The main features are as follows:

- Categorization with 95% accuracy
- Filters and themes
- Large-scale processing of messages
- Conversations
- Monitoring
- KPI measuring
- Real-time analysis with drill-down functionality
- Out-of-the-box integrations

These features enable you to do the following:

- Capture relevant data only
- Automatically filter data received
- Automatically categorize data
- Listen to social conversations and understand sentiment
- Automatically route social conversations to appropriate teams
- Track the progress of social conversations
- Monitor relevant insights and drill down for more information
- Use KPI measuring to improve your social engagement
- Issue stronger marketing messages
- Have better service adoption
- Have fewer defects in services or products

Conclusion

Oracle Social Cloud enables your company to collaborate effectively, both internally and externally, and become a social company in which every part of your company influences your objectives.

Oracle Social Cloud is integrated out of the box with Oracle Sales Cloud, Oracle Marketing Cloud, Oracle Service Cloud, and Oracle Commerce Cloud, enabling you to constantly innovate and find new ways to move your business objectives forward.

Summary

In this chapter, we have covered the most important Oracle CX solutions available at the time of writing. Oracle is constantly expanding its CX offerings with best-of-breed products, which means that functionalities can overlap, but each of them shines in some aspects.

It is imperative that you understand the needs of your company so that you can choose and combine solutions that will best suit your needs.

To summarize, you can use products for these purposes:

- Oracle Sales Cloud—Central CRM-like solution
- Oracle Marketing Cloud—Manage your campaigns
- Oracle Service Cloud—Contact center solution and self-service solution
- Oracle CPQ Cloud—Pricing and quotas solution
- Oracle Commerce—Storefront, sites, and B2B/B2C solutions
- Oracle Social Cloud—Social engagement tool

In the next chapter, we will learn about the CX solution architecture and its implementation.

CX Solution Architecture

3

Solution architecture is the method by which value is delivered to an organization. It encompasses solution inception, solution design, and solution implementation. To be able to achieve appropriate solution architecture, the full business context needs to be understood and documented as a part of the solution inception effort. Solution design investigates and elaborates on possible options, and delivers the implementation plan. The solution implementation phase communicates the plan to the business and guarantees appropriate implementation processes and outcomes.

The topics covered in this chapter are as follows:

- Understanding the CX architecture
- Exploring the logical view
- Oracle CX products

Understanding the CX architecture

Customer experience (**CX**) is a new concept, and is currently garnering a lot of attention from the business community worldwide. CX encompasses all interactions and experiences that a customer has with a brand, company, or product. CX utilizes the all-channel experience, and it includes all interactions across a set period of time.

The most important metric for CX is an overall experience that is a combination of digital and physical environments.

A goal of CX is to tailor a consistent, personalized, and efficient experience in every contact with the customer. Mastering that interaction can foster brand loyalty and help develop word-of-mouth natural marketing.

The Oracle CX offering enables companies to design the best possible customer experience and to utilize closed-loop reporting to make improvements in each new run of the process.

Solution architecture

In this chapter, we will focus on possible CX solution architectures. To be able to do so, first, we need to understand what **Solution Architecture** actually is.

Solution Architecture is the process of designing, describing, and implementing the solution related to specific business problems:

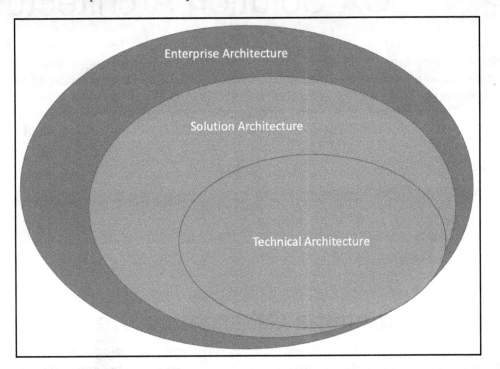

As we can see in the preceding diagram, **Solution Architecture** is a subset of an enterprise solution architecture, and it encompasses **Technical Architecture**. **Solution Architecture** is a connection between **Enterprise Architecture** and **Technical Architecture**. Solution architecture is focused on details and solution technologies, while technical architecture only focuses only on technical aspects.

Well-defined solution architecture addresses the problem in an appropriate manner, so that it fulfills requirements defined by the business.

The main objectives of solution architecture are as follows:

- Match with the corporate/company environment.
- Fulfill stakeholders' requirements.
- Understand and address project constraints.
- Utilize appropriate technological solutions.
- Address non-functional requirements.

Solution architecture is the basis for any IT project, since it is a framework that aligns business goals with technology, resources, and skills.

Customer journey mapping

The purpose of solution architecture is to fulfill business requirements. To be able to do so, we need to define requirements that this solution must provide. Our best tool is customer journey mapping, since it will outline customers' communication points with the company and customers' points of view, which will help us to make a list of requirements that the solution must fulfill.

The following is a simple example of customer journey mapping:

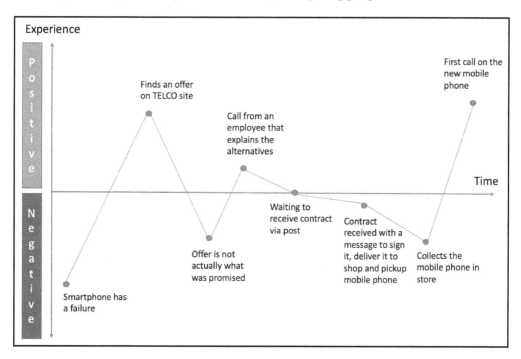

If we were to define requirements from this customer journey mapping, we could assess that our solution architecture must fulfill these requirements:

- A better explanation of offers on the company site may include a chatbot, so that the customer gets all the relevant information in a single visit.
- The process of signing a contract and receiving a mobile phone must be simplified.
- There should be no visit to the TELCO (Telecommunication) store.

CX reference architecture

For companies to be able to address new and changing business requirements, they first need to address their own IT infrastructure. **Business support systems** (**BSS**) are usually silos containing different parts of information and functionalities, resulting in a non-unified experience for the customer. The silo effect prevents the company from achieving a truly cross-channel customer experience solution.

The architecture will be described in a general way, and we will outline possible integrations with Oracle CX to provide existing solutions and will outline end-to-end solutions.

Deployment type

Companies today, especially corporations, have strict guidelines on how and where to deploy solutions. The first question that should be answered is which type of deployment will be needed, since it will greatly influence our solution architecture.

Usually, we can split possible deployments into four categories:

- A public cloud platform is accessible and open to the public, to individuals or organizations, and is owned by a company that sells cloud computing services. In the case of public platforms, the question of the security of personal data is raised. Apps from different users are often located on the same servers, storage systems, and networks. Public clouds reduce security risks and costs by providing a variable infrastructure. They make the temporary leased infrastructure of the organization. If the public cloud is implemented with a performance-oriented focus, the security and location of other applications launched on the cloud should not create problems with the cloud architecture and end users.

One of the benefits of public clouds is that they can be much larger than private clouds. Public clouds offer the ability to increase or decrease the leased part of the cloud, and shift responsibilities, if unplanned risks arise, from the organization to service providers. Public cloud components can also be under the exclusive use of only one user, making a private data center. However, incorporating images of virtual machines into the public cloud does not provide insight into the cloud infrastructure, while leasing data centers gives users greater insights into the infrastructure itself. Then, users can manage not only virtual machine images but also servers, storage systems, network devices, and network topologies. Creating a private virtual data center with components in the same object reduces the problem of having a multitude of different data locations, because the upload speed is much larger when connecting objects within the same cloud. This kind of offering usually utilizes a pay-per-usage model.

The following diagram outlines how public clouds are utilized. All four companies are connecting to the same cloud, but each of the companies are sandboxed, so that there are no interactions between the data or processes of each company:

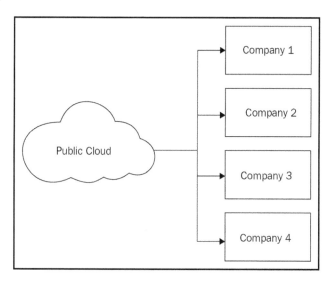

- A **Private Cloud** is available to one organization only. It can be managed by the organization itself, or by someone else. Organizations use private clouds when they need or want more data control than they can get by using public clouds. Private clouds are designed solely for the use of a single client, giving them the highest degree of data control and the highest level of security for the data on the cloud. The organization has the infrastructure, and has control over the distribution of applications on its own infrastructure. Private clouds can also be deployed within the organizational data center. IT service companies, or service providers, build and manage private clouds. Organizations that have a private cloud can install programs, apps, store data, and can manage the cloud structure. Private clouds also provide companies with a high level of control over the use of cloud resources.

The following diagram outlines how private clouds are utilized. Company PCs are connected to the cloud, and consume the cloud's resources. Only PCs that are a part of that company can access the private cloud's resources:

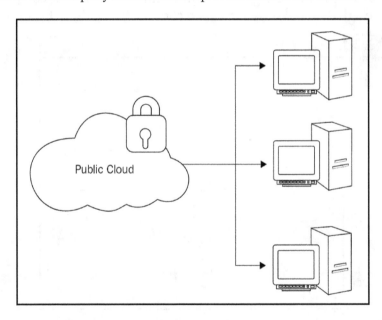

- Managed services demand that the business should outsource certain processes and systems. The goal of managed services is for the company to attain up-to-date technology, have access to skills, and address problems associated with value, quality of service, and risk, because the IT infrastructure elements of the many **small and medium businesses** (**SMB**) and enormous companies are migrating to the cloud, with **managed services providers** (**MSPs**) facing the challenge of cloud computing more and more. A variety of MSPs are providing in-house cloud services, or are acting as brokers with cloud services suppliers. The absence of information and experience in cloud computing, rather than the companies, reluctance, seems to be the main obstacle for the companies making transition.

The purpose of managed services is to enable companies to always have the latest technology, and the know-how associated with it, without the investment in the hardware or people required to run the service. Companies providing this service are called MSPs. MSPs can manage in-house systems and processes, cloud-based systems, or a combination of both. Usually, MSPs also take care of communication with the cloud provider. MSPs remediate the main problem with the adoption of cloud-based solutions—a lack of knowledge and experience—since the company is purchasing this service from the MSP.

The following diagram outlines how the managed services model is utilized. The company consumes cloud resources, and it is on premise infrastructure as a service. All maintenance and configuration are outsourced to the managing company:

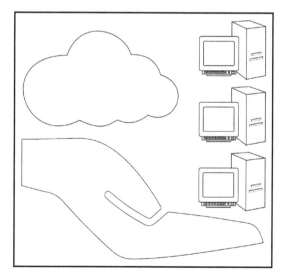

- On premise is a traditional method employed for the running of enterprise software, which means that the company owns and runs the software on its own servers.

The following diagram outlines how the on premise model is utilized. The company is managing all of its infrastructure and PCs:

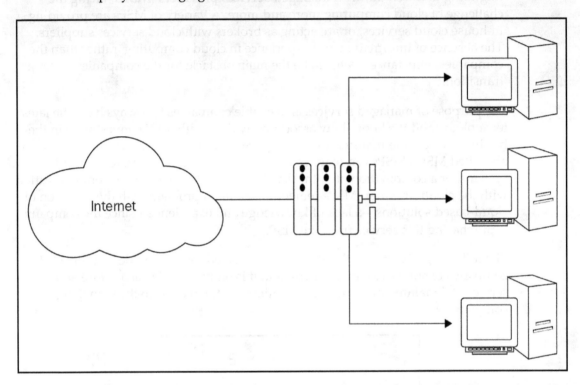

These categories are not exclusive, and usually, for best results, they can be combined and we can use a hybrid approach to solution architecture.

- Hybrid clouds can also be used to manage large planned loads. While private clouds can be used to perform periodic tasks that simply divide same workloads between on premise and public clouds, hybrid clouds encounter the complexity of determining how to distribute public and private cloud applications. In addition to this problem, you must also take into account the relationship between data and resource processing. If the data is small, or the application does not remember the condition, the hybrid cloud may be a better solution than copying a large amount of data into a public cloud (where simple processing is performed).

Principles

The purpose of principles is to define a framework that facilitates the transition of business requirements into IT solution definitions. These principles are generic, and are on the solution level, while functional requirements can be per one system, or part of a solution.

Components

According to **The Open Group Architecture Format** (**TOGAF**), the best practice for writing down components is to describe them with these four topics:

1. **Name**: This should outline the essence, be easy to remember, and should not contain technological information.
2. **Statement**: This should describe a fundamental statement in easy-to-understand terms.
3. **Rationale**: This should describe business benefits using business terminology. Also, it needs to describe relations with other principles.
4. **Implications**: This should highlight business and technical requirements, including resources, costs, and tasks. From the implications, the reader needs to understand the answer to the question, *How might this affect me?*

Quality

For principles to be usable, they need to adhere to the following five criteria, so that quality and usefulness is assured:

- Understandable
- Robust
- Complete
- Consistent
- Stable

Examples of architecture principles

Now, we will define principles to which the solution needs to adhere. Each table consists of one principle with these rows:

- **Name**: The name of the principles
- **Statement**: Business requirements
- **Rationale**: Why a company should do it
- **Implications**: How implementing this principle will influence the business and its customers:

Name	Unified customer experience
Statement	Functionalities and responsibilities across all channels must be defined.
Rationale	The company must provide consistent and seamless interaction across all touch points with the customer.
Implications	The customer will have the same experience, not influenced by a type of touch point.

Name	Easy to use
Statement	The solution is easy to use for customers and employees.
Rationale	The more time that is needed to invest in understanding applications, the more time those users need to invest in understanding how to use applications, and the less incentive they have to use them.
Implications	The solution must adopt a common look and feel, encompassing all of the components of the solution.

Name	Maximum benefit
Statement	Decisions are made to provide maximum benefit to the enterprise.
Rationale	Decisions made for the benefit of a whole enterprise have higher values than decisions made for the benefit of a single part of the organization.
Implications	Priorities for solution definition and adoption must be established for the enterprise as a whole.

Name	Security first
Statement	A comprehensive and centrally administered security solution is needed.
Rationale	Non-centralized security without a unified view and reporting increases the risk of security incidents.
Implications	The company will need to implement centralized security and **identity and access management (IAM)** solutions.

Name	Integrations
Statement	All of the systems incorporated in CX solution must be integrated so that they are able to provide unified experience for customers and gain a unified view about them.
Rationale	Integrations need to adhere to SOA principles, so that they are able to support the changes to support agile businesses needs in an appropriate manner.
Implications	Shift from system-centric to a customer-centric mode.

Name	Omni-channel support
Statement	Functionalities should not be unique to a specific channel—they should be general in nature.
Rationale	**Time to market** (**TTM**) is much lower if functionalities are general in nature. Functionalities are the same across all the channels.
Implications	Common monitoring and management solutions need to be implemented for each of the channels. The functionalities defined need to be feasible across all the channels.

Exploring a logical view

The purpose of the logical view is to outline what functionalities a solution provides to end users. In our case, we will use them to represent the whole customer life cycle, alongside the company's business processes:

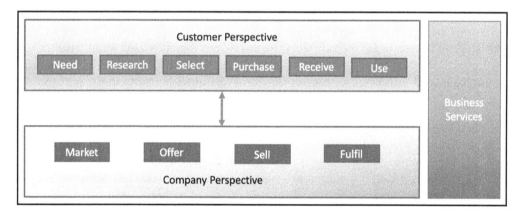

Business Services, comprising BSS systems, are tasked with supporting a unified customer experience across all of the channels throughout the customer journey.

One important aspect that is not within the control of companies, and that is missing in our first diagram, is social media. This represents another touchpoint that we need to consider in our architecture, so we are going to add it to our high-level architecture:

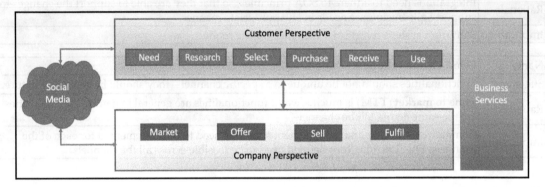

Let's now move on to understanding their architecture.

Logical architecture – commerce components

The main feature of our solution architecture should be that all information and functionalities are available from all relevant devices, such as laptops/PCs, tablets, and smartphones. Solutions must include the customer's perspective, and must tend to customer needs, such as searching, browsing, viewing a product/service, selecting a product/service, and purchasing product/service. Additionally, our solution should provide assistance to customers so that they are able to make informed decisions.

We also need to address customer experience from a look-and-feel point of view. We must ensure that our pages look nice, while also being easy to navigate and use. Another functionality that we need to provide is recommendations based on a variety of variables known about the customer, the customer's history, and other customer information from the same segmentation.

At the point when a customer decides to purchase a product or service, we need to ensure that pricing and an accurate inventory state is presented to the customer. All information that a customer needs must be available in real time.

Support systems need to be able to fulfill and provide orders in an appropriate amount of time, be it activating/deactivating services, or sending the product from the warehouse.

Throughout the customer journey, all information must be collected and available for analysis, so that the company is able to personalize the experience, and understand hidden opportunities.

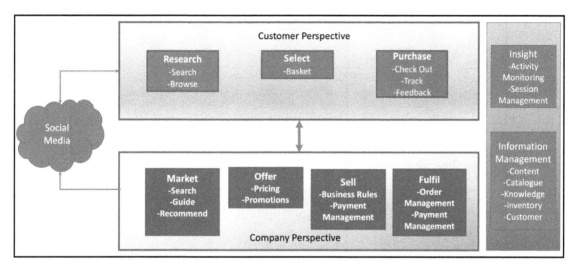

Keeping all of these requirements in mind, we are now able to expand our solution architecture as shown in preceding image.

Logical architecture – loyalty and marketing components

When considering marketing and loyalty, the primary factor to take into account is product marketing. A goal of product marketing is to design and implement a consistent and all-encompassing experience across all devices. In our consideration, these components are part of the **Need** and **Recommend** phases.

The main goal of marketing is to create a need for services and/or products, with the goal of establishing customer loyalty. The best indicator of customer loyalty to a company is through word-of-mouth recommendations about a company's services and products.

Communication via social media needs to be a two-way interaction. Social media enables companies to build engagement and promote a company's services/products, depicted as follows:

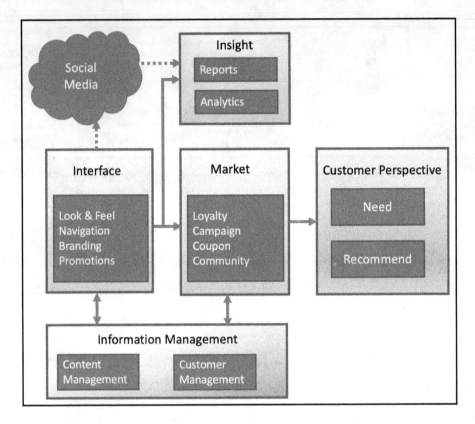

A company must be able to utilize the data gathered through marketing activities, and tailor campaigns that increase brand loyalty using promotions through all available channels.

The goals of loyalty and marketing are to coordinate a considerable number of people across the company so that the following can be achieved:

- Customer acquisition
- Customer retention

With that in mind, we will need to change our solution so that we are able to address these two goals.

Logical architecture – service components

The main purpose of this solution architecture is to provide self-service functionalities, including all information regarding orders to customers. Another objective is to provide support to a customer, that is accessible through any communication channel that the customer would like to use. Examples of such help include a knowledge base, chat-functionality integrated communications, ticketing systems, and guided help.

The following diagram shows this:

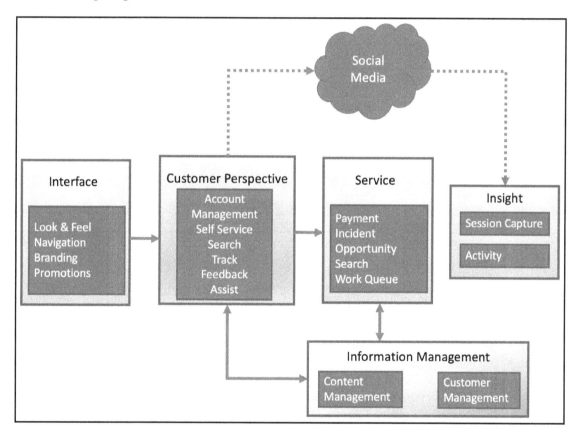

Similar to other solution architectures, all information gathered from any interaction across any channel needs to be analyzed.

Logical architecture – reference architecture

In previous sections, we have described a solution architecture focusing on specific areas. Our goal now is to describe a unified architecture covering all business requirements, vertical emphasizing maintenance requirements, and horizontal business requirements.

The architecture covering all business requirements is as follows:

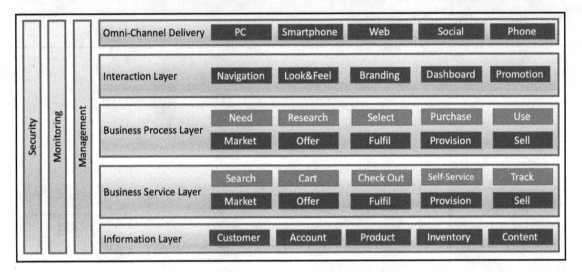

From the preceding diagram, we can observe the following:

- **Omni-Channel Delivery** describes all the channels available in our solution. Experience is consistent across all of the channels.
- The **Interaction Layer** outlines functionalities that must be aligned so that experience is the same across all of the channels.
- The **Business Process Layer** describes business processes that will be available and conducted by our solution. Green (dark ones) processes are from a customer's point of view; grey ones are from the company's point of view.
- The **Business Service Layer** describes services that are needed to support processes. White services are from a customer's point of view, grey ones are from the company's point of view.
- The **Information Layer** describes information that is needed for services and processes.
- **Security**, **Monitoring**, and **Management** are all-encompassing and are needed so that our architecture is secure and operates in the best possible manner.

Oracle CX products

Until now, we have been describing the logical architecture of our solutions. The next step for us is to map these logical architectures to our products. An important thing to keep in mind is that this will not be a one-to-one mapping, since one product is usually comprised of multiple sets of functionalities:

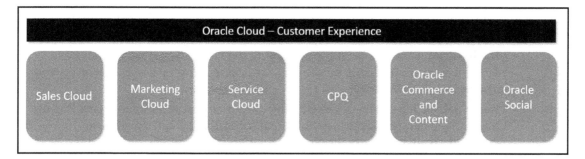

The products that we will use in our solution architectures are marked as follows:

- **Oracle Social Cloud**: This enables your company to collaborate effectively both internally and externally, and become a social company in which every part of your company influences your objectives. Oracle Social Cloud offers out-of-the-box integration with Oracle Sales Cloud, Oracle Marketing Cloud, Oracle Service Cloud, and Oracle Commerce Cloud, enabling you to constantly innovate and find new ways to drive forward your business objectives.
- **Oracle Commerce Cloud**: This is an extensive and unified solution for companies with B2B and B2C business. It has a myriad of advanced features, and, when paired with other solutions in Oracle CX, offers benefits and contributes to the overall architecture representing your storefront.
- **Oracle CPQ Cloud**: This is a process within the sales life cycle. Each business that sells complicated products incorporates a **configure, price, and quote** (CPQ) method in one way or another. Once a client is curious about a product, the salesperson should put together the quote to satisfy the customer's request.
- **Oracle Service Cloud**: This provides companies with a unified interface, which enables them to monitor and engage with customers over any channel that is available to them. Since it is a part of the Oracle CX suite, it enables you to easily integrate with other offerings and unlock the full potential of your CX environment.

- **Oracle Responsys**: This is used to manage and orchestrate marketing interactions with customers across email, mobile, social, display, and the web.
- **Oracle Eloqua**: This is used for marketing automation; that is, for creating personalized campaigns across multiple channels. Oracle Eloqua comes with the support of 500 partners, and comprises 700 integrations, which can be used in your campaigns.
- **Oracle BlueKai**: This is used for marketing data management. It enables you to understand the data that you have gathered in your campaigns. Essentially, it is a cloud-based big data platform.
- **Oracle Infinity**: This is used for marketing data analytics. It is an analytics platform used for tracking, measuring, and optimizing visitor behavior on your sites and apps.
- **Oracle Sales Cloud:** This is Oracle offering the closest resemblance of CRM in Oracle CX. It can be used as a standalone solution, and can do all tasks reasonably well; but the real power of the Oracle CX suite is unlocked if it is paired with other solutions.
- **Oracle Right Now Web Experience**: This is a self-service platform, which enables your customers to manage their options, subscriptions, contact data, submit cases, and so on. What they can manage depends on your design. The perfect design would be to allow customers to change their subscription. Subscription should be stored in Oracle Sales Cloud, and when the customers log in, it should be acquired using an API call and presented to the customer, alongside all subscriptions that the customer can migrate to. The last step should be the customer's verification of change, and a data change in Oracle Sales Cloud through an API call.
- **Oracle Right Now Contact Centre Experience**: This functionality enables you to manage communication with customers through a unified interface. If paired with Oracle Field Service, it can help you to facilitate communication between your technician teams and customers.

Commerce solution

We will show how the functionalities outlined in commerce logical architecture can be represented with Oracle CX products:

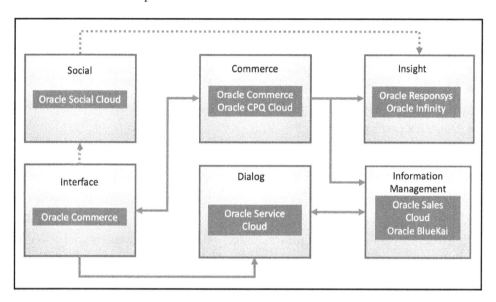

Social provides a company with social tools, facilitating the flow of information between customers and the company in real time. The company is able to publish information, conduct marketing campaigns, engage with customers, and manage their brand on social networks. **Social** also provides the company with the option to understand customer sentiment, and act on this in a timely manner.

The **Interface** uses the storefront functionality of the **Oracle Commerce** cloud. The storefront (entry) can be easily customized and expanded, so that it can suit your business needs. A guided search enables customers to find all relevant information in a simple and easy way. The storefront functionality supports your B2B and B2C business.

Commerce utilizes the **Oracle Commerce** and **Oracle CPQ Cloud** solutions. Some of the benefits of these are listed as follows:

- Enables your company to manage promotions
- Uses payment gateways
- Uses integrated reports
- A social plugin can share information on social networks
- The company is able to configure and maintain products and services
- Manage cross-sell and up-sell
- Create offers based on region
- Complex pricing rule
- Dynamic promotions based on defined variables and order executions

In the case of complex sales or discounts, the company can utilize a built-in approval engine. Engagement can also be configured so that it is administrated by AI using machine learning.

The dialog uses, unifying all your communication channels into one channel in one user interface. Your agents will be able to see all of the cases and communication, supplemented with information from all systems outlined in this solution.

Insight uses **Oracle Responsys** and **Oracle Infinity**, providing business with the ability to collect data, draft reports, evaluate and augment data, and analyze data. This can be used to create personalized campaigns, create customer journeys, and increase customer value.

Information Management uses **Oracle Sales Cloud** and **Oracle BlueKai**. Information management will enable the company to create a 360° view of all customers, enrich data, accurately identify customers across devices, share the data with other solutions, and record the data on the basis of device ID. You can also define custom objects in **Oracle Sales Cloud**, while maintaining clean and accurate data.

Loyalty and marketing solution

Loyalty and marketing solution will focus on providing your business with marketing and loyalty features, such as campaigns, promotions, and coupons:

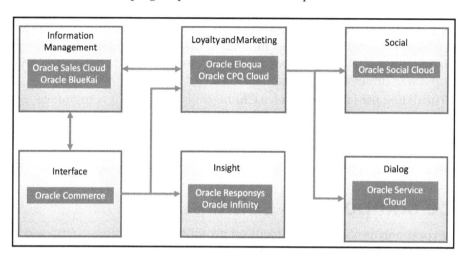

Let's understand what is happening here:

- **Information Management** uses **Oracle Sales Cloud** and **Oracle BlueKai**. Information management will enable the company to create a 360° view of all customers, enrich data, accurately identify customers across devices, share the data with other solutions, and record the data on the basis of the device ID. You can also define custom objects in **Oracle Sales Cloud** while maintaining clean and accurate data.

- The **Interface** uses the storefront functionality of **Oracle Commerce** cloud. The storefront can be easily customized and expanded so that it can suit your business needs. A guided search enables customers to find all relevant information in a simple and easy way. Storefront supports your B2B and B2C business.

- **Loyalty and Marketing** uses **Oracle Eloqua** and **Oracle CPQ Cloud**. This enables your company to automate and personalize marketing activities. To be able to do so provides your company with advanced segmentation and targeting, lead management, sentiment analysis, adaptive campaigns, closed-loop reporting, web analytics, the ability to create offers based on region, complex pricing rules, dynamic promotions based on defined variables, and order executions. In the case of complex sales or discounts, the company can utilize a built-in approval engine.

- **Insight** uses **Oracle Responsys** and **Oracle Infinity**, providing the business with the ability to collect data, draft reports, evaluate and augment data, and analyze data. This can be used to create personalized campaigns, create customer journeys, and increase customer value.
- **Social** provides the company with social tools, facilitating the flow of information between people and companies in real time. The company is able to publish information, conduct marketing campaigns, engage with customers, and tend to brand on social networks. **Social** also provides the company with the option to understand the sentiment, and act in a timely manner.
- The dialog uses **Oracle Service Cloud**, unifying all your communication into one channel in one user interface. Your agents will be to see all of the cases and communication, supplemented with information from all systems outlined in this solution.

Service components solution

The service components solution will focus on providing your business with service features, such as incidents, guided help, and self-service for customers:

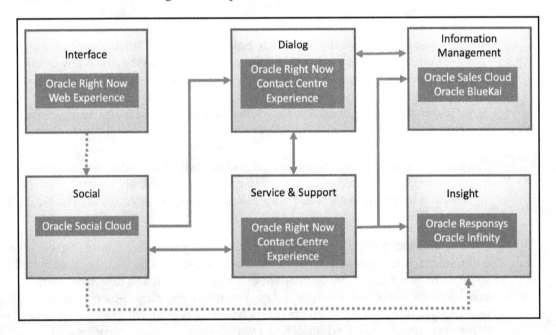

Let's understand what is happening here:

- **Interface**: Interface uses **Oracle Right Now Web Experience**, which allows your customers to access self-service tools, access forums, use an interactive guide, get answers from intelligent auto-response, use the knowledge base, and provide feedback. Syndicated knowledge only shows information that is relevant to web page content. All of these features can be accessed from any device. On the occasion that the customer wants to contact your customer support, they can do so via email, chat, cobrowse, or they can phone agents seamlessly from the page.
- **Social**: Social provides the company with social tools, facilitating the flow of information between customers and companies in real-time. A company is able to publish information, conduct marketing campaigns, engage with customers, and tend to brand on social networks. Social also provides a company with the option to understand the sentiment and act in a timely manner.
- **The dialog uses Oracle Right Now Contact Center Experience**: This, in a nutshell, is a cross-channel contact center. This enables your customers support to manage cases through any channel, support customer to a guided resolution, and engage customers proactively using a unified desktop application for your agents. All of these functionalities are configurable to tend to your business needs in the best manner.
- **Service and Support**: **Information Management** uses **Oracle Sales Cloud** and **Oracle BlueKai**. Information management will help a company to create a 360° view of all customers, enrich data, accurately customers across devices, share them with other solutions, and the data on the basis of a device ID. You can also define custom objects in **Oracle Sales Cloud** while maintaining clean and accurate data.
- **Insight**: This uses **Oracle Responsys** and **Oracle Infinity**, providing businesses with the ability to collect data, draft reports, evaluate and augment data, and analyze data. This can be used to create personalized campaigns, create customer journeys and increase customer value.

Security and monitoring

Since our solutions are in a cloud, the best way to provide security, monitoring, and **single sign-on** (**SSO**) is to utilize Oracle's offerings.

Oracle Identity and Access Management

Oracle Identity and Access Management (IAM) enables companies to achieve single sign-on and identity management throughout all applications. It issues, validates, and exchanges security tokens across all solutions.

The functionalities provided by Oracle IAM are as follows:

- Authentication and SSO
- Real-time risk identification
- Fine-grained authorization
- Web services security
- Security token services

Oracle Enterprise Manager

Oracle Enterprise Manager enables companies to manage all cloud solutions from one cloud-control user interface.

Functionalities provided by Oracle Enterprise Manager include the following:

- System monitoring
- Compliance management
- Cloud management
- Hybrid cloud management
- Application management
- Database management
- Middleware management
- Life cycle management
- Application performance management
- Application quality management
- Life cycle management

Preparing for implementation

Before starting the implementation of your new architecture, there are some prerequisites that need to be considered:

- Assessing processes and procedures
- Assessing IT infrastructure
- Assessing which of your existing software will be retained
- Assessing users and roles
- Preparing data
- Setting up reporting

The purpose of IT solutions is to support business processes and procedures. Understanding them creates a baseline for your implementation. It is important to understand which existing IT solutions with corresponding processes will be removed, and which ones cannot be removed and so need to be integrated and adjusted to support new solutions.

The usual reason for implementing new solutions is to support new processes and procedures, which means that new user groups with appropriate roles and privileges need to be created. In this phase of planning, security must be on top of the list, and the principle of least privilege should be asserted.

For a new solution to operate optimally, data must be prepared. Data that has no value should be removed, and data quality and accuracy must be assured.

The last task should be to outline reports. Reports are one of the most important aspects of any solution, and having appropriate reporting may be the difference between successful and unsuccessful implementation.

Going through these steps will enable your organization to successfully adopt new solution architecture, without having any negative effects on the running of your business.

Summary

Today, it is becoming increasingly difficult to distinguish your company from all of the competitors. Moreover, this is a constant activity, and companies need software that will enable them to do so in an appropriate manner. Solutions and architectures described in this chapter are the tools that you need to succeed in this environment, offering companies building blocks that are interchangeable and configurable to address the ever-changing needs of your business. A considerable number of functionalities are shared between solutions, which means that they are more or less building blocks that enable you to reorganize your processes in a situation of organizational change.

In our solutions, we have covered commercial capabilities, loyalty and marketing, service and support, social engagement, and a 360° view with enhanced data and analytics.

Combined, all of these functionalities will enable your business to thrive and adapt to any, and every, challenge that it can face.

In the next chapter, we will discuss how to gather requirements, document existing processes, and design new processes, both organizational and technical.

Section 2: Service Provisioning and Basic Settings

In this section, we will understand how to put together and deploy the Oracle CX suite, and we will provide a list for As-Is and To-Be analysis. Then, we will learn how to adopt CX in several schemes, before finally seeing how to organize CX projects with different frameworks.

The following chapters will be covered in this section:

- Chapter 4, As-Is and To-Be Analysis
- Chapter 5, *Adopting a Strategy - Organizational Changes*
- Chapter 6, *Organizing and Conducting an Implementation Project*

4
As-Is and To-Be Analysis

Business analysis deals with rules and assumptions using an analytical way of thinking. The integration of information technologies with business processes requires an analysis of business processes, and often requires the re-engineering of these processes. A formal approach is needed to ensure an optimal level of process design and implementation.

Business models are used as abstractions of complex business realities and serve as a basis for business analysis. Under the concept of business analysis, we analyze existing *(As-Is)* and future *(To-Be)* business processes of the organization in order to improve the performance of the company.

The main objectives of this chapter are to describe the analysis process and its delivery, and we will also cover the following topics:

- The purpose of business analysis
- Understanding business processes, tools, and methods
- Understanding As-Is analysis
- Understanding To-Be analysis

All of these topics will enable us to understand the importance of As-Is and To-Be analysis processes.

Technical requirements

No software installation is required for this chapter. This chapter will cover the theoretical background needed for understanding the role of each CX Suite.

The purpose of business analysis

The prerequisites required to understand the As-Is and To-Be analysis is what we are going to study in the following sections. Here, we will study why business analysis is important as well as looking at how it fits into the scope of business processes and, ultimately, the scope of the As-Is and To-Be analysis. To understand these analyses, we will understand business notations with the help of supporting diagrams which led us to these analyses.

Business analysis provides a structured approach to the introduction and management of organizational changes. It is used to identify and define the need for change in an organization model and to facilitate their implementation.

Business analysts are involved at all levels of an organization, from defining a strategy, creating a company architecture, taking the lead in defining project goals and requirements, and participating in continuous improvement in technology and processes. Business analysts are actually a link between business users and IT—they are best placed to understand the business and its problems, and thus they ensure the quality of the services provided.

Business analysis directly influences the success of a project as it reduces the main factors that are the cause of project failure by:

- Improving the quality of requests (detailing what needs to be done, as better requests provide better output) and improving communication within teams.
- Increasing the speed and quality of delivery
- Contributing to customer satisfaction
- Improving change management

Thus, business analysis affects the quality of the delivered product as well as the reduction of costs incurred in the production process. Every change should result in the company performing better, and so business analysis is the first step that you need to take in order to improve.

Let's see how that applies to an organization...

Successful organization management and, in particular, raising the efficiency of the company for the benefit of reaching set goals, is only possible under the assumption that there is excellent knowledge of its internal organization and mode of action. The activity of an organization is realized through a series of related and goal-oriented business processes. A complete business process definition will be provided in the next section, but for now, it can be considered that a business process is a set of related work steps for which it is possible to determine the duration of the execution and the required resources.

The organization's effectiveness can be enhanced by improving and reorganizing business processes. However, it is imperative for all participants to fully understand business processes, which will be possible if they are described in an unambiguous and comprehensible way. Business processes and their correlation in performance can be described using various techniques. Natural language descriptions are certainly one way to describe business processes, but they may be inaccurate, and could expose the participants to different interpretations of the processes. Therefore, business processes are precisely described by means of a set of graphic symbols, with exact definitions of semantics and solid rules around their connection.

It should be noted that each process can have its own processes; that is, each process follows a higher-order process. This way, you can perform a review of a very complex process on more than two hierarchical levels, provided that all the rules that apply to the two-level hierarchy are respected.

It is recommended that such structuring is carried out so that at one level there are no more than 10 activities at one time.

Understanding business processes, tools, and methods

To achieve an appropriate analysis of business processes through an objective approach to researching and analyzing, it is first necessary to define what these are. Generally, two types of definitions are used when identifying and analyzing business processes—descriptive and genetic.

Business process analysis is a continuous process that usually consists of five steps—**Design**, **Modeling**, **Execution**, **Monitoring**, and **Optimization**. This process can be seen in the following diagram:

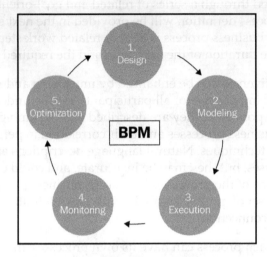

Any job that is done in an enterprise or institution can be considered a business process. However, should this definition be further explored and promoted, it is necessary, at least temporarily, to adopt a definition that is involved internally with the process and provides answers to the following questions:

- What is the purpose of existence of the process?
- What are the reasons and the goals of the process?
- What is the history of the process?
- What is its inner structure of the process?
- How does the process work and under what conditions does it work?
- What resources are needed for the process to work? Who are the participants in the process?

The answer to these questions is the so-called **genetic definition**.

According to the genetic definition, a business process is a connected set of activities and decisions that are driven by an external incentive to achieve a measurable goal of the organization. Business processes take input information or resources, and after processing them, the input is converted into specific products or services important to the customer or user. Let's consider that this definition works, and note that toolkit manuals that supports business process modelling use mostly similar, but incomplete, definitions.

Let's analyze this definition in more detail, as follows:

- **A connected set of activities and decisions**: It is understood that this is a deliberate set of actions and decisions (not a conglomerate) that lead to achieving goals and meeting the customer's or user's needs.
- **Running on an external incentive**: The organization does nothing and does not waste any resources if there is no demand or incentive from a customer or user. In manufacturing organizations, this incentive is a customer's order, though it does not always have to be immediate, and can be planned (which depends on the production management system).
- **Specific products or services**: Each process output result must be individually recognizable (meaning that no other process should produce the same outcome) and measurable.
- **Of importance to the customer or user**: An organization that existed for itself would not make any sense; a company exists only for its customers or users of its products or services. However, in complex organizations whose activities are organized on the value chain principle, the customer or user does not always have to be external, but may be some internal organizational unit.

It should be emphasized that this definition of a business process should be formally understood only to some degree. Practice shows that great effort in modeling is useless if, at the very beginning, no processes have been identified that fit this definition.

Basic elements of business processes

In order for a process to be analyzed and improved, it is necessary to have an unambiguous definition, but it is also necessary to unambiguously describe all relevant business process properties. This is so that every possibility of a different interpretation of the process is excluded. It is necessary to use a solid formal language that will enable a thorough and objective analysis of the business process and its systematic improvement.

A convenient way of describing a business process is a graphical representation, especially if it is supplemented by a formal description of certain features. Business people, executives, analysts, and information system designers have long been using different systems for graphical business presentations.

In order to definitively avoid the possibility of different interpretations, and to enable computer-based management of business processes, standards are defined that prescribe the mode of presentation, and description of processes and their relationships. The most recent and most commonly used standard is called **Business Process Modeling and Notation (BPMN)**, and the process of applying it to business and IT domains has been named the modeling of business processes.

BPMN is a graphical standard for business process modeling prescribed by the **Object Management Group (OMG)**. One of the goals of the BPMN standard is to provide a business modeling notation that is understandable to all interested parties. BPMN allows business analysts to define complex business processes from start to finish.

The basic diagram of standards is called the **Business Process Diagram (BPD)**. It shows the management and data flow of business processes. In addition to the BPD, the BPMN standard consists of three different diagrams, as follows:

- A choreographic diagram
- A diagram of a collaboration
- A diagram of conversations

The BPMN standard is very complex, and has around 100 different concepts. Thanks to its large number of concepts, processes can be modeled in detail.

It should be noted that each process can have its own sub-process – that is, that each process can be a process in a higher-order process. This way, you can perform a review of a very complex process on more than two hierarchical levels, provided that all the rules that apply to a two-level hierarchy are respected. It is recommended that such structuring is carried out so that at one level there are no more than 10 activities.

Types of business processes

Every company generally relies on three types of processes. These are:

- Essential processes
- Support processes
- Management processes

Let's understand each process one by one.

Essential processes

Essential processes are the most important processes in any company, and they are usually the ones that are used most frequently. We could also call them core processes, since the successful running of these processes is essential for the wellbeing of the company.

Examples of essential business processes are as follows:

- The running of marketing campaigns
- Fulfilment
- Order management

The advantages of essential processes are as follows:

- Generating profit
- Providing benefits to customers

Supporting processes

The purpose of **supporting processes** is to support operational processes. These processes are not designed so that they can generate profit, but they assure the smooth running of the business.

Examples of supporting processes are as follows:

- Hiring new employees
- Logistics
- Facility which houses the company

Supporting processes are general processes, that is why they are usually not directly connected to the company's core business.

Management processes

Management processes are responsible for business development and growth. They are usually divided by the time periods that they encompass.

Examples of management processes are as follows:

- **Strategic planning**: 3, 5, and 10-year plans
- **Tactical planning**: A yearly plan
- **Operational planning**: Daily activities

Management processes define essential processes, the running of which will be enabled by supporting processes.

Management processes are usually outlined in four steps, as shown in the following diagram:

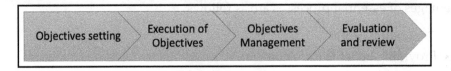

These processes are usually defined and implemented by the highest level managers.

Business process notations

Until the emergence of business process notations, models were implemented in different ways. The consequences of this were that different approaches delivered different results. Companies were not able to deal with a multitude of combinations of notations. Without a unified and structured approach, it is very difficult to harmonize the needs of business systems and business processes which, in practice, leads to many irrational solutions and failures, and often causes the inefficient implementation of ICT solutions.

Therefore, the need for a structured and unified approach is an essential prerequisite for the successful implementation of any solution.

In this section, we will discuss two widely accepted notations, BPMN and UML. We will gain an understanding of the Ishikawa and Pareto diagrams as well. This is the prerequisite knowledge required for us to dive deeper into the chapter.

BPMN

BPMN was designed with the aim of making it understandable to business users and technical personnel alike. BPMN provides a standardized way to coordinate business process design and process implementation tasks. The goal of BPMN notation is to facilitate a unified graphical representation of processes.

Generally, according to BPMN, processes can be divided into two categories, external and internal, from a company's perspective.

External processes are related to processes in the company environment and their communication with the organization. Internal business processes include basic processes, support processes, and management processes. If the focus is only on internal business processes, it is generally assumed that the company is only concerned with the internal functioning of the company, and is not considering the impact on the customer. The basic goal of modeling an integrated management system is the definition of its structure and the establishment of links between internal processes. Expanding web technologies are conditioned by the significant cooperation of business partners, suppliers, and users.

Based on this, BPMN notation has the ability to present businesses through visually designed, standardized, business processes representation, and to enable the concept of business integration.

A business process can also be understood as a service consisting of sub-services, in which internal and external business relationships are defined. These relationships need to be integrated. Usually, a business process contains several other relationships.

A business process map consists of the following:

- Actors
- Activities
- Events
- States

BPMN coordinates processes by coordinating messages that are exchanged between different business participants.

A business process has three parts—entry, procedures, and exit. Components of a business process must be arranged according to the type of data and the semantics of the business premises over which the data is transmitted.

BPMN notation implies the following three basic types of business processes:

- Internal processes
- Abstract processes
- Global processes

BPMN provides guidelines on how to enhance business process modeling, detailed here:

- It is better to organize distribution and training in terms of notation, as well as in terms of business designers and analysts. This form of modeling is very much sought-after and current in all world organizations. The notation is simple and quick to learn, which is its greatest advantage.
- Work on improving BPMN 1.0 specifications relating to innovative and creative additions, or changes to particular elements of notation, especially when modeling collaborative business processes.
- Take advantage of translating the BPMN business process diagram into executive languages.
- Finally, the application of BPMN notation in design and executive business sectors should be harmonized at all hierarchical levels.

UML notation

The **Unified Modeling Language** (**UML**) is a set of graphical notations that help us describe and design IT systems. It is definitely handy to know that UML makes considerable use of a block and line form, and line variations and arrows are often used to distinguish between different types of links.

We will describe three out of nine UML notations:

- Class diagrams
- Use case diagrams
- Activity diagrams

Class diagram

The UML class diagrams provides and narrates the class description as well as the interactions between them, especially those based on the relationships and the concept of inheritance.

In the early stages of design, attribute details and operations can be omitted or restricted to the minimum number, which is according to the requirement constituting the most apt logical concept, embedded in a particular class. In later phases, when design verdicts are concluded, a description can be extended. From the point of view of the model, description is one element that is used for a constructive view and deals with the connections between implementation elements, but on a large-scale.

Use case diagram

Although the concept of scenario utilization is and informal way to determine how the system will be used, with respect to the whole idea and the role it plays in the design process, this results in a more general concept of use cases. The analogy between connection utilization/scenarios and program/thread execution is possible.

In this context, the execution shows a general set of possible actions, while the thread is one instance of this process, so use cases describe a set of viable interactions between the system and the other participants (people, hardware, and so on), while the scenario describes a definitive progression of these interactions. The UML use case diagram describes this thought at a rather general level.

Activity diagram

An activity diagram is one way of modeling the all-important dependencies and sequences that surface when an operation has multiple goals.

An activity diagram is consequently desirable for modeling the type of coordination required where a process cannot be continued until certain conditions are met (for example, new data is available). So, states in such diagrams now represent expression execution or action execution, and the focus is on triggering a transition between the states of such a system, and thus synchronizing and coordinating different actions.

Understanding fishbone diagrams – Ishikawa diagram

A fishbone diagrams, also known as **Ishikawa diagrams** or **cause and effect diagrams**, is a tool that helps us to identify and understand possible problems. The following diagram shows the relationship between causes and consequences:

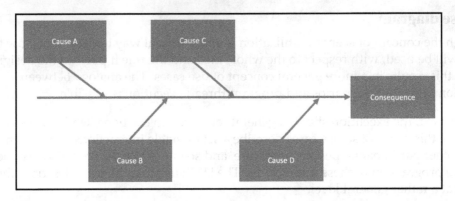

When drawing a cause and effect diagram, the participants construct a graphic representation of the causes, organized to show their relationship with a specific consequence. The image in *The purpose of business analysis* section of this chapter shows the basic structure of the diagnosing cause and effect. It should be noted that the diagram has the cause and side effects included.

The process of steps for constructing and analyzing a cause and effect diagram are as follows:

1. **Consequence identification**: First, select areas or issues that need to be analyzed. From these, extrapolate consequences, and describe and group them. Use definitions – define the consequences within the team to ensure that they are clear and unambiguous. Results can be positive or negative. Negative results are usually described as problems, and positive results as targets. It is paramount that you establish a positive atmosphere, since it encourages participation and honesty. Whenever possible, it is recommended to express the consequences in a positive way. Do not focus only on negative aspects, since it can steer the team to focus only on justification, and it creates a blame game environment. Another possible approach is to encourage the team to focus on problems; this approach can also lead to a positive outcome. The best approach is to let the team decide on the approach.

2. **Draw the consequence**: Using a tab or larger sheet of paper that is displayed so that each team member can see it well, write a brief description of the consequences or outputs that are the result of the process.

3. **Identify the cause**: Identify the main causes that contribute to the consequences we are analyzing. These are the causes that will become a category in your diagram, on which you can list other causes connected to category. This will enable you to find other causes and highlight the connections between them. You should make an inscription on the diagram for the category makes more sense.

4. **Identify other important factors**: Identify as many of the possible factors and links between them. After identification you can link them to the main branches. Describe them in a detailed manner. If one of the lower-order causes is connected to higher-order causes, specify it as a branch of the higher-order cause.

Example of Ishikawa diagram analysis

Let's go through a real-life use of an Ishikawa diagram on a simple **personal computer (PC)** performance troubleshooting example.

First, let's think about possible causes of why a PC may slow down. We can group the causes into the following four categories:

- User
- Software
- Hardware
- Surrounding

This provides us with enough information to make the first draft of an Ishikawa diagram, shown as follows:

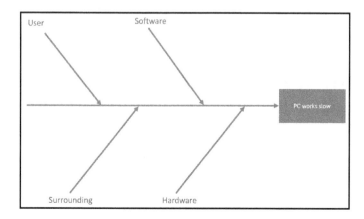

We have defined four causes that could have led to the consequence.

The next step is for us to expand on each of the causes, as follows:

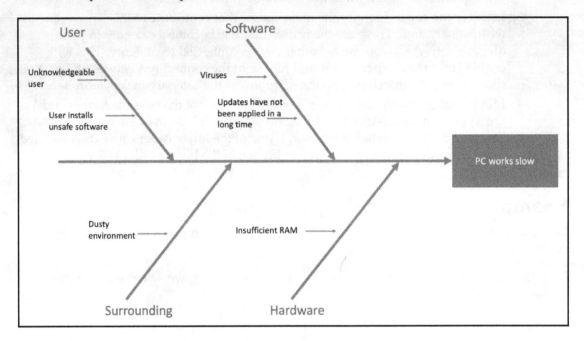

From this diagram, we can see all the possible reasons why the PC is running slowly. If observed correctly, we can see that *User installs unsafe software* and *Viruses* are connected issues appearing in two causes. This means that a lack of user knowledge has introduced viruses to the PC, which is the most probable explanation of why the PC is working slowly.

The fishbone diagram, or causes and effects diagram, only gives an overview of the possible causes of the problem, which means that you will also need some other tools to improve analysis, for example, using a Pareto diagram.

Understanding Pareto diagrams

Pareto analysis, named after the Italian economist Vilfredo Pareto (1848-1923), was developed as a diagrammatic method of grouping the causes of a problem according to their relative significance. It represents the process of selecting priority problems for solving. One of the best and simplest ways to differentiate the most important problems from the rest is the application of the *ABC* method, devised by Vilfredo Pareto.

The application of this method is very broad—it is used in exploring the possibilities to reduce losses, reduce congestion in the production process, rationalize the consumption of materials, researching the viability of the production program, study the work of application, and so on.

The basis of this method is based upon the idea that a small number of significant causes are accompanied by a myriad number of insignificant causes. Often, more than half of the properties of one problem are the result of the same cause.

In such a situation, a much better approach is the localization and elimination of the most important causes, and then attempt to eliminate all the causes at the same time.

Eliminating an important cause will result in a drastic increase in quality with minimal effort. With this connection, in Anglo-Saxon literature, the 80/20 rule is very often discussed. For example, 80% of the problem occurs in 20% of devices; or employees. Or 80% of the welfare of society is concentrated in 20% of the population.

A Pareto diagram can be used either with quantitative or attribute data, but is most often used with attribute data. Usually, these figures are expressed in percentages. For example, the available data can be grouped in such a way that it becomes clear that many product malfunctions are caused by several causes.

The good thing about the Pareto principle is its universality, which means that you can apply it everywhere, in all areas and industries, for example:

- Project management
- Sales
- Marketing
- Working with clients
- Improving the work process

It is always applicable everywhere, in any branch of the industry, for both personal and business goals. When you have multiple activities to complete, always complete the ones that will help you to achieve your personal and business goals first. 20% of these activities will help you to achieve 80% of your goals. So always ask yourself, *does this help me to achieve my goal, and to what extent?*

Some examples of using the Pareto method are as follows:

- Identifying the most important customers
- Identifying the most important customer needs
- Determining the most important categories of complaints about the service
- Determining the skills that are needed for the employees
- Tracking the cost of failures

Example of Pareto diagram analysis

When using a Pareto diagram, the first step is to make a list of complaints and the number of their occurrences during a specific time period. The only tool that you need is Excel, which has a built-in Pareto diagrams function in its statistical chart's functionalities.

Let us see how to do this:

1. First, we make a simple list in Excel, as shown in the following screenshot:

Customer Complaints	
Complaint	Count
Complaint 1	27
Complaint 2	680
Complaint 3	65
Complaint 4	8
Complaint 5	14
Complaint 6	28
Complaint 7	16
Complaint 8	111
Complaint 9	39
Complaint 10	595

2. After that, we can select `Complaint 1` to `595` and then select the Pareto diagram function in the **INSERT | statistical charts** menu. As shown in the following screenshot, it will create a Pareto diagram:

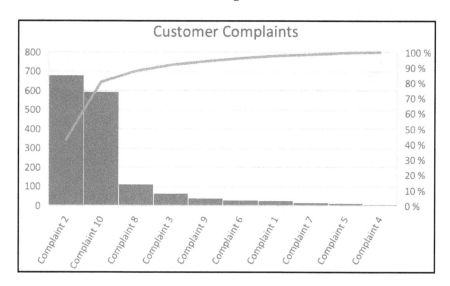

Abiding by the 80:20 rule, we can deduce that *(680 + 595)/1583 =0.805*, or approximately 80%, which means that `complaint 2` and `compliant 10` are causing 80% of the issues for the customers. Therefore, the company should focus its efforts on the remediation of those two issues.

Diagram analysis

The analysis helps you identify the causes that justify further research. Since the cause and effect diagram identifies only the possible causes, project teams should use the Pareto diagram to determine the main cause that they should focus on first. An important point to consider is the appropriate level of detail when describing the issues. All issues should be described at a similar level, allowing us to conduct further research in the appropriate area.

If the main category has only a few specific causes, it usually indicates that a further identification of causes is needed. If one main junction has only a few related sub-divisions, the appropriate course of action is for them to be grouped into one category. Look for repeated causes in different areas. Repeated causes usually represent the root of issues. Establish measurements for each cause so you can quantify the consequences of any changes you might make. After establishing metrics, identify and solve the causes that you can take action on.

Understanding the As-Is analysis

Implementing new systems and solutions in corporate environments is not as easy as initially turning on the server. The implementation process takes a lot of time and effort. The cornerstone for successful implementation is to be able to understand the current situation, which is why the first step in any implementation needs to be an As-Is analysis. Failing to understand the basis of this analysis can lead to organizational disruption, decreased productivity, and exorbitant costs. This is usually caused by a less than optimal business processes definition, which implies less than optimal performance of implemented systems and solutions.

Steps in As-Is analysis

CX projects, by nature, are process improvement projects, which means that the goal of As-Is analysis is to examine every aspect of processes that will be changed or replaced. The purpose of As-Is analysis should be to create a visual diagram that explains and determines possible areas of improvement, while containing required associated text and metrics. When improvements are identified, the To-Be analysis can then be conducted.

The usual steps of conducting an As-Is analysis are as follows:

1. Defining flow charts and recording business processes using UML or BPMN notation
2. Acquiring an understanding of possible improvements and root causes, explained with fishbone diagrams

Gap analysis

Delivery of As-Is analysis can be in the form of gaps, BPMN diagrams, Pareto diagrams, and fishbone diagrams, which combine the need to present a unified view of the company with the focus on customer-facing processes.

Good analysis should clarify the following points:

- Clarify the company's stance regarding CX
- Clarify what is currently being done right, and what is missing or being ignored
- Clarify and quantify the impact of these deficiencies on the business
- Clarify gaps from both the customers' and employees' perspective
- Clarify overall qualitative and quantitative impacts

To be able to do this, it is imperative to structure the gap analysis appropriately and have sufficient time and resources. The best practice in gap analysis is to hire external resources, since that will provide an impartial view of the company and facilitate interdepartmental cooperation.

Tools and methods that can be used to achieve this are as follows:

- **Interviews**: One of the most useful methods of gathering information regarding CX gaps is interviewing key employees across the company. These employees are domain experts, usually aware of the difficulties that customers face and the internal challenges that are preventing the company from providing an appropriate customer experience.
- **Internal reports**: These can provide a deep understanding of how the company conducts its own business and what the values and KPIs are that are important to the company. Gap analysis can conclude that metrics used in reports need to be changed to facilitate CX implementation.
- **Market research**: Market research reports usually contain customer feedback, with their views and experience regarding products or services provided by the company. They also can outline the company's focus on specific market segments.
- **Customer interactions data**: Usually, the company has a wealth of data regarding customer issues as a result of contact with their customer service team. This information is usually not analyzed and utilized appropriately. This is usually because of complex interdepartmental relations and conflicting objectives. The objective of this exercise should be to impartially assess and bring to light customer issues.
- **Customer journey mapping workshops**: These workshops should be conducted with interdepartmental resources, and they should highlight different customer's experiences interacting with the company.

GAP analysis usually results with a large number of GAPs identified. GAPs need to be identified and constructed so that they can be understood as part of the processes in BPMN/UML notation, and connected to root causes in the fishbone diagram. Also, to be able to address gaps in an appropriate manner, their impact should be quantified. Some low-level gaps may be omitted from a project plan or placed in subsequent phases.

Deliverables

A product of As-Is analysis should be a combination of BPMN/UML, fishbone diagrams, and a GAPs list. Having these documents will enable you to have an appropriate view about the state of your business at any point in time.

Service activation example

Here, we will outline a simple example in which a TELCO company is addressing one of the causes of customer dissatisfaction. The issue is first recorded as a gap:

Nr.	GAP description	GAP	GAP Severity Minor/Normal/Major	GAP Priority 1-5 (1 Highest, 5 Lowest)
1.	Customers wait more than 3 days to have network equipment replaced. During that period they are not able to use the company's services. Current replacement time is estimated to be 7 days.	4 Days	Major	2

In the preceding example, we can see that it requires more than three days to replace network equipment for a customer, which leads to customer dissatisfaction.

Now let's study a BPMN process example

This process outlines the flow of events that happen when the customer raises a support request for the replacement of equipment. The diagram shows the interaction between the **Customer**, **Contact Center** department, **Field Service** department, and respective IT systems:

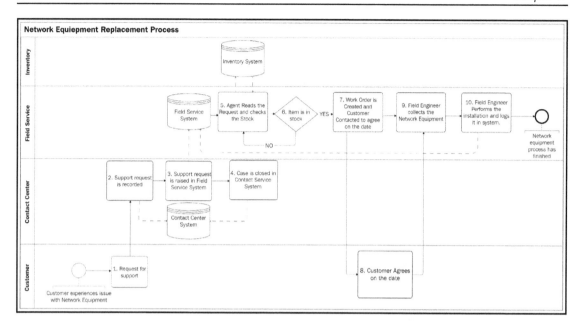

In the following fishbone diagram we will note all of the causes that lead to a consequence. The diagram shows four types of causes that all contribute to one consequence. Each cause has further information:

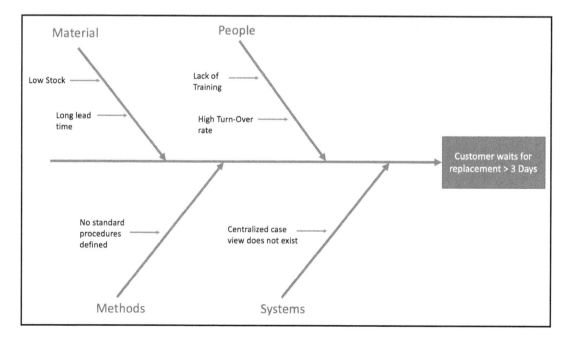

The following Pareto diagram outlines which issues will remediate 80% of the customer complaints:

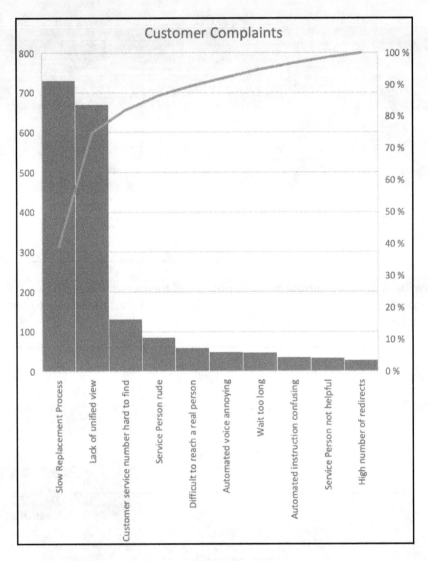

This section has outlined the As-Is analysis for a BPMN using a fishbone and Pareto diagram.

Understanding the To-Be analysis

To-Be analysis defines the future state of a business process in a company. The goal of this analysis is to outline how future business processes will work, and what changes need to be implemented. These analyses should encompass all aspects of the company, including systems and processes alike.

Companies usually conduct As-Is analysis and organize a project to address the gaps outlined in the analysis. To be able to conduct an implementation project in an appropriate manner, To-Be analysis needs to be define and should be one part of a project.

The starting point of To-Be analysis should be As-Is analysis. As-Is analysis should outline which gaps should be remediated, but To-Be analysis should also address the company's strategies and goals.

The prospect of doing a To-Be analysis may seems overwhelming if done in a big-bang fashion. The best approach is to define the To-Be analysis with an accompanying plan using a series of small improvements.

Generally speaking, To-Be analysis is needed if your project has one of the following aspects:

- The project impacts the business processes
- The project improves the business processes
- The company is deploying new solutions and the business needs to adapt
- The company is deploying a new service or a product and the business needs to adapt
- The deployment of new solution or system is influencing existing processes

The delivery of the To-Be analysis should consist of the following:

- Defined processes to be implemented
- Organizational changes needed to support the processes
- Solution implementation/changes plan
- Financial analysis
- Explained benefits
- Project plan

The most important aspect of To-Be analysis is to secure a sign-off and mandate from all of the affected shareholders. Failing to do so will surely result in an unsuccessful project.

Summary

An appropriate business analysis provides a structured approach to the introduction and management of organization changes. It is used to identify and define the need for changes in an organization's model, and to facilitate their implementation.

Business analysis is involved in all levels of an organization, such as defining strategies, creating the company's architecture, and taking the lead in defining project goals and requirements. As such, it is essential for the continuous improvement in technology and processes, providing a link between business users and IT.

Appropriate analysis directly influences the success of a project, as it reduces the main factors that are the cause of project failure such as speed, quality of delivery, and customer satisfaction, while also improving change management.

Thus, business analysis affects the quality of the delivered product and reduces the costs incurred in the production process.

In the next chapter, we will discuss the next step in the adoption of a CX solution – that is, planning the strategy and what to consider when doing so.

5

Adopting a Strategy - Organizational Changes

The word *strategy* refers to the *game plan* of a company, and **strategic management** is defined as a set of measures and actions that result in formulating and implementing a strategy designed to achieve the goals set by the organization. It is a continuous process of adjusting the environment to suit the purposes and objectives of the system, which increases the readiness and ability of the company to respond to the events in an appropriate way. This reduces or eliminates resistance to changes in the environment, something that often increases the differences between the company's capabilities and the demands of the environment.

Customer Experience (**CX**) implementation projects are usually hindered by resistance to changes from within the organization. It is essential that the implementation plan addresses this aspect with utmost diligence. Managing the strategy implementation process requires a good mix of the various factors and elements that contribute to the achievement of strategic goals.

The implementation process can be facilitated by certain factors. The question is how to diagnose and find those factors that will have a decisive impact on the quality of the process. The issue is even more complex if you analyze the scope and variety of problems that arise in the process. Therefore, it is necessary to focus on those elements that actively participate in the implementation and try to see what is needed for them to do so.

The implementation process is handled by *middle-management* employees. Employees at this level receive the tasks (strategies); they are in charge of organizing the implementation process.

When it comes to complex activities, it is necessary to develop organizational knowledge that will help achieve the goals, that is, find help outside the organization if the organization's knowledge is not sufficient.

This chapter will cover the following topics:

- Understanding strategic management
- Implementing a strategy
- The process of implementing a strategy
- Understanding the CX-specific strategy
- Elements of a CX strategy

Understanding strategic management

Strategic management, which includes strategy formulation, performance, performance evaluation, and control, allows you to study and evaluate opportunities and threats in the business environment, taking into account your own capabilities and weaknesses.

Based on the definition and characteristics of strategic management, it can be concluded that this is a concept that ensures the company is appropriate in a face of changes in the business environment.

Strategic management consists of a series of steps, namely these:

1. Conducting environmental and business analysis
2. Establishing company guidelines
3. Formulating the company strategy
4. Implementing the strategy
5. Monitoring the implementation to adapt to the changes that are made within the strategic control process

Steps 1, 2, and 3 fall into the formulation stage, and steps 4 and 5 fall into the implementation stage.

The strategic management steps are cyclically repetitive—which means that decisions are made based on a trial-and-error approach:

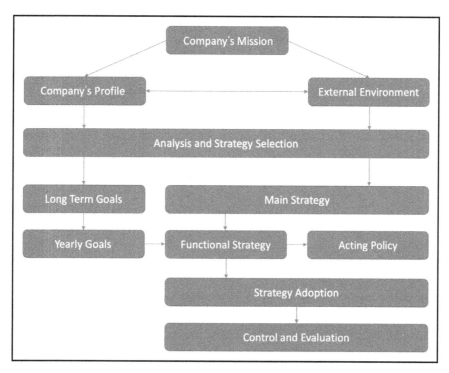

This diagram outlines how the company's mission is distributed, from top to bottom. It also shows that the two most important factors in each strategy should be the company's profile and external factors. Furthermore, it highlights what the main strategy is, and the yearly goals are variables that need to be taken into the account when drafting a functional strategy. The strategy adoption process needs to be controlled and its outcomes evaluated.

Implementing a strategy

The strategy must be implemented as a foolproof action, which can be broken down into three stages:

- Identifying measurable commonly set annual goals
- Developing special functional strategies
- Developing and binding concise policy-making, for decision-making

Yearly goals

Annual goals represent concrete, measurable plans for what an organizational sub-unit should do to contribute to the fulfillment of the main business strategy. Annual goals focus on implementation through the transformation of long-term goals into concrete and short-term goals. While such goals clarify the long-term purpose(s) of the main strategy and the basis for assessing the success of the strategy, they are less useful for guiding operational strategies and the current actions needed to implement the main strategy.

One annual goal must be clearly linked to one or more long-term goals of the main business strategy. To achieve this, it is of great importance to understand how to differentiate between two types of goal.

Here are four differences between annual and long-term goals:

- **Timeframe**: Long-term goals are usually implemented over a period of five years or more. Annual goals are more immediate and usually take place over a period of one year.
- **Focus**: Long-term goals are based on the future position of the company in its competitive environment. Annual goals determine the specific tasks of the company, areas of activity, or other departments, in the following year.
- **Concern**: Long-term goals are broadly defined (not so specific), while annual goals are very specific and are directly related to the company, a specific area of activity, or other departments.
- **Significance**: While long-term and annual goals are quantitatively determined, long-term goals are expressed in broad, relative terms, for example, *the market share is 20%*. Annual goals are expressed in absolute terms, for example, an increase in sales by 15% in the following year.

The implementation of the main strategy requires coordinated intrinsic goals. Successful implementation of the strategy depends on the coordination and integration of the operational units. This is facilitated through the creation of short-term (annual) goals. Also, the implementation of the strategy requires consistency of the annual goals. Annual goals are more consistent if each goal is clearly stated, that is to say—what to do, when this is to be done, and how to evaluate what is being done. These goals can then be used to monitor the effectiveness of one operating unit and, collectively, the progress toward the long-term goals of the business.

Successful implementation requires year-to-year measurability. This is usually achieved by emphasizing the importance of measurable activities, and then acceptable and measurable results are determined.

The second important quality of the annual goals is related to the need to prioritize short-term goals. When developing annual goals, the time needed and the impact that they will have on the successful implementation of the strategy should be considered. In terms of the time, this means that one activity finishes before the next one starts. All annual goals are important, but some deserve additional attention owing to their special impact on the success of the strategy. If these goals are not indicated, this may be because conflicting assumptions about the relative importance of the annual goals undermine progress toward strategic effectiveness.

Advantages of following strategic goals

The systematic elaboration of the annual goals allows managers to turn the long-term goals and the main strategy into activities:

- Annual goals enable operational managers and members of staff to better understand their roles within the company
- If these goals are achieved with the participation of the managers responsible for their implementation, then they give an *objective* basis for the related conflicting political interests that may interfere with the effectiveness of the strategy

Effective annual goals become an essential link between strategic intent and operational reality. Well-set annual goals provide the basis for controlling the strategy.

Functional strategy

A **functional strategy** is a short-term plan related to the key fields of the actions of a particular company. Such strategies explain the main strategy by giving more concrete details of how to work on the key areas of action in the near future. Action strategies must be developed for key marketing, finance, manufacturing, research and development fields, and staffing.

They must be aligned with the main strategy. They help implement the main strategy by organizing and activating specific departments of the company (marketing, finance, manufacturing, and so on) to track the business strategy related to daily activities.

Action plans

Action plans are instructions that managers need to follow in order to implement their organization's strategy. They consist of guidelines that outline how to act in certain situations, raising the companies' efficiency while keeping activities aligned with operational strategy.

Action plans provide managers with a mechanism for avoiding hasty or bad decisions about changes that need to be made in some activities. Action plans can be formal and in written form, and they can be non-formal and conveyed orally. The reasons for informal (unofficial) and oral plans of action are usually related to the strategic need for secrecy in relation to competitors. In some cases, unwritten informal plans of action may hinder the long-term success of the strategy. However, managers and employees usually love the freedom that is gained when the plans of action are informal.

The process of implementing a strategy

The process of implementing the company's strategy involves the harmonization of strategy and organizational structure, the design of an appropriate management system, and the corresponding organizational culture.

The three organizational factors that provide basic and long-term funding for the institutionalization of an enterprise's strategy are as follows:

- The enterprise's structure
- The leadership and key managers
- The enterprise's culture

The conditions for successful strategy implementation entail shaping of the organizational structure and organizational culture.

Organizational structure and processes definition

The **organizational structure** is designed to ensure that tasks, technologies, and people are used in the most efficient way to achieve the mission of the organization. The structure provides managers with a way to balance the following two conflicting things:

- Dividing tasks into logical groups
- Integrating these groups to ensure the efficiency and effectiveness of the organization

Structure determines the executive, managerial, and administrative organization of the firm, indicating responsibility and hierarchy. This affects the flow of information as well as the context and nature of the interactions among people. The organizational structure is usually described in terms of its dimensions—centralization, formalization, and complexity. The complexity of the organization's structure is reflected in the following:

- **Horizontal differentiation** is the extent to which the tasks of a particular organization are divided into homogeneous groups
- **Vertical differentiation** refers to the number of levels in the hierarchy of a particular organization
- **Spatial dispersion** reflects the extent to which a particular organization has few or many locations, as well as its overall geographic scope

Formalization of the organizational structure reflects the extent to which rules and procedures govern the activities of a particular organization. Formalization can be a double-edged sword. On the one hand, this can reduce the uncertainty and confusion over the powers and responsibilities to the minimum; on the other hand, it can limit individual discretion, risk-taking, and innovation. Formalization differences are usually quite different among functional fields and the hierarchical levels in an organization.

The centralization of the organizational structure is the extent to which the powers of decision-making at higher management levels remain within one organization. Although it provides an important means of coordinating decisions, it can also put excessive demands on executives at the top. Together with the growth of the organization in size and scope, their decision-making activities must be decentralized.

The main types of structure are simple, functional, divisional, and matrix. Keeping hold on companies and multinational structures can be considered departmental variations. Dimensions and types of structure are linked to the organization's strategy and are interrelated. Each type of structure is acceptable under certain conditions and has certain advantages and disadvantages.

The formation of the organizational structure and process flows through organizational methods and approaches. We also use organizational profiles in the form of different views. In the method of organizational structure and process design, we use methods of analysis and the shaping of organizational structures and processes.

The process of shaping or supplementing the organizational structure and processes flows through the following steps:

1. Recording the current state
2. Analyzing the current structure and processes

3. Designing new structures and processes
4. Implementing new structures and processes

The responsibility for shaping changes in organizational structures is the management of the company. The degree of complexity and the extent of the change depend on whether these issues are handled by upper management or middle management. In the case of changing the overall organizational structure, the inter-connectedness of individual parts in the organizational structure would be handled by upper management. Smaller changes to the organizational structure of departments or services are middle-management tasks. In any case, upper management must be familiar with the changes to approve them.

The results of the organizational structure and the process-shaping phase are changes in the organizational structure and processes that are aimed at supporting the implementation of the company's adopted strategy.

When it comes to strategic management, the design of the organizational structure comes in two levels:

- The first is related to the analysis of the state of the enterprise. The existing organizational structure is one of the most important factors in the phase of determining its capabilities.
- The second phase of shaping the organizational structure and processes is related to the phase of shaping the company's strategy.

Based on the accepted strategy of the company, we have to establish the scope of organizational changes, to support the company's strategy.

Organizational culture

In addition to the organizational structure and processes for the successful implementation of the company's strategy, there is also a significant correlation between strategy and organizational culture. Organizational culture represents a set of basic assumptions that the group through the learning of the process, addresses the interference of external adaptation and the internal integration of the enterprise and presents them with the new member as the right way to find out and solve the problems mentioned.

Put simply, organizational culture is also defined as an integral system of norms, values, performances, assumptions, and symbols that determine the way of behaving and responding to the problems of all employees and hence shaping the appearance of an enterprise.

In addition to the previously mentioned coverage, organizational culture is of great importance as well, as it involves new associates in the company. Everyone who joins the company should understand the organizational culture; that makes the culture of the company a management tool that ensures better employee engagement.

Analyzing and shaping organizational culture requires a systematic approach. In most cases, such an approach consists of the following:

- Analyzing the existing organizational culture
- Evaluation stages, where we find the disagreement between the existing organizational culture and the company's strategy
- Phases of design, through which we change or support the existing organizational culture

We use the analysis of the existing organizational structure, which is similar to the analysis of the organizational structure, for the development of organizational culture profiles. Based on the created profiles of the existing and necessary organizational culture, we carry out an assessment of the consistency between the existing and the necessary organizational culture. Based on mutual comparison, we form the necessary measures to preserve and strengthen the existing organizational culture or to change and actively shape new organizational culture.

Implementing process-tracking

We have taken control of a management function, and it is, by the classic concept, the last in a series of functions to be performed in the management guidance process. Its task would be to compare the rate of achievement of the set goals by comparing the planned and achieved goals.

The best possible approach to control starts with the following assumption that each control process as a management function consists of three steps:

1. Measuring results
2. Comparing the results to the standards that were set
3. The preparation needed to perform the measures to achieve the set goals

The essence of the control process is the comparison of the achieved results to the set goals and the design of the elimination measures.

The control function of the strategic management process involves four types of control:

- Strategic control
- Enforcement control
- Prediction control
- Preventive control, specific to the individual

In every form of control over the action of the strategy management process, we have to go through the following steps:

1. Evaluating the results (qualitative and quantitative methods of measurement)
2. Comparing the results to the set goals and requirements
3. Shaping the measures to eliminate deviations

The shape of the entire control system depends on whether we perform the supervisory function for each phase of the strategy management process or for the work process, such as the phase of forming the company's strategy. Compared to the results obtained, we use very diverse comparative reports, such as government reports and branch business reports. For the objectivity of the evaluation of results, we rely on the strategic review of external experts.

Understanding the CX-specific strategy

A change in the ways of interacting with your customers arose from a change in the buyer-seller model. This change started in the 1970s and continues to this day. From the year 2000 onward, the model became more complex, due to the rise of the internet, followed by social media and general advancements in technology. So, today we need to consider the customer a primary asset.

So, the business needs to consider the following:

- Customer satisfaction should be more important than developing good products and services
- Existing customers need to be retained
- The customer must have a *great brand experience*
- There needs to be a better relationship between the customer and the company

Focusing on the individual needs of a particular type of customers requires a specific set of values. Customer loyalty and satisfaction are the most important goals now; products and services are secondary. Companies that prosper are the ones that are able to maximize the value of their existing customers while acquiring new customers in a stable and predictable manner.

The purpose of CX strategy

The purpose of CX strategy should be this—to be different than your competition. This can be done by being able to deliver the best possible mixture of values and experiences to a customer in deliberate and informed manner.

To achieve this, the business needs to be able to achieve the following:

- Create a distinctive value proposition
- Tailoring the activities to suit the value chain
- Choose what not to do
- Spread the strategy over the appropriate parts of the organization
- Create continuity in your approach

Customer-first processes are at the center of the modern business strategy. The best companies know how to leverage CX technology, align it with their processes, and achieve the best possible business outcomes. It is especially important that the CX strategy is helped and not hindered by the implementation process of a CX solution. CX strategy needs to be split into steps that are achievable and not detrimental to the bottom line and customer experience.

A good strategy should be split into these five steps:

1. Creating a value proposition
2. Tailor appropriate communication
3. Handling trade-offs
4. Determining organizational fit
5. Enabling continuity

We will now discuss each of these steps.

Creating a value proposition

The **value proposition** in broad terms can be expressed as a reflection of the choices that the company makes. The basic consideration of each CX strategy plan should be the customer's point of view. The following is a very simple depiction of this:

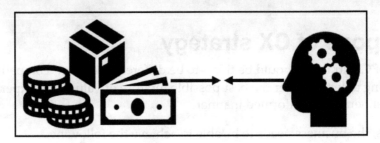

To be able to offer the best value to your customers, the company should be able to answer the following three questions:

- Who are our customers?
- How do we meet our customers' needs?
- What is our profit margin?

To answer these questions, we need to explain them further.

Each industry has different customers. The first step in building a good relationship with customers is acquiring an understanding of which customer segmentation helps the company to achieve business goals. Segmentations can be understood as a group of like-minded people interested in achieving the same goal. The objective of the company's strategy should be to create a platform that enables these groups of people to exist and engage. As the customer at the center of the strategy, it is paramount to select appropriate segments to engage them. Analysis of this segmentation should be done with value and profitability in mind. A business strategy needs to be aligned with the target customers' needs and products and services pricing.

The company needs to be able to build a strategy based on unique abilities that meet customers' needs and decide which resources to market. Initially, established target segmentations need to be expanded and updated as a result of data collection and analysis.

The viable pricing of products and services is one of the primary indicators of effective customer relations. The company needs to analyze sales data from target segments and align pricing with the customers' needs. This will enable the company to unlock its hidden potential.

The last thing to consider regarding value is offering something to potential customers that the company's competitors do not offer.

Tailoring appropriate communication

The best outcomes of communication come when the adopted communication plan is similar to the company's competitors' plans, but conducted in a different way. CX and processes that the company adopt during the implementation enhance the communication between the company and the customers. Some of the channels that CX provides are marketing automation, email, social, and so on. The company needs to tailor the communication activity so that it strengthens the value proposition:

Good customer relations are adjusted to reflect the sentiment of the primary customer segment. The CX solution should be able to communicate your stories using images, words, and themes associated with human interactions. Social engagement allows this type of communication to be viral and tailored to specific customer and present value proposition, in a personal and relatable manner.

The appropriate communication plan is a connector between your company's business activities and your customers; therefore, your communication should also encompass internal and external communication.

Handling trade-offs

Handling trade-offs essentially means how to choose which actions not to take and accepting limitations. This is a critical process to master for any successful strategy implementation process. Choosing a *hand-off* usually can be described as a fork in the road, as you cannot simultaneously select both ways—you need to choose one:

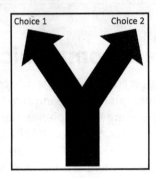

We can use the customer service department as an example of a CX strategy having trade-offs built in. In this case, the company can focus only on supporting a primary segment of customers or having a multi-tier approach toward customers. A trade-off, in this case, means that customers who are not in the company's primary segmentation will probably not remain loyal to the company, but you will increase the loyalty of your primary segment customers. Another benefit is that it will enable customer services to focus more on important cases and to have fewer cases overall. Another aspect of the appropriate CX strategy is to listen to your customers' complaints, but your company cannot focus on all complaints, so the trade-off is to listen primarily to complaints coming from your primary segmentation group and not give too much attention to other complaints. This will enable the company to focus on important complaints, but it will probably lose customers belonging to other segmentations.

So, CX strategy means that doing everything for all customers comes with a sizeable financial loss. CX strategy should address all of these aspects and select the appropriate trade-offs.

Determining organizational fit

For a strategy to be successful, it needs to be connected to business activities. Essentially, this means that a strategy cannot be connected to a single business competence, rather it needs to be connected to and rely upon the magnitude of other business competencies. **Company** and business processes need to be aligned with a communication strategy:

CX **Strategy** is a management choice that enables the various business processes, departments, and stakeholders to fit together. It is paramount for management to determine the company's **return on investment** (**ROI**) to measure the effectiveness of the company's CX strategy. The definition of ROI must correlate to the adopted proposition value and the processes that support it.

As the old saying goes—*a chain is only as strong as its weakest link*. In our case, this means that, for the CX strategy to be successful, employees, marketing activities, and employers all need to be aligned to the same goal, and the measurement of success must take all of this into account.

Enabling continuity

The adopted CX strategy must be consisted over time. Without consistency and continuity, a company is not able to implement the strategy over a long period. Therefore, the CX strategy needs to be flexible and ready to adopt the changes that will arise over time. This is how we want it to be—in harmony:

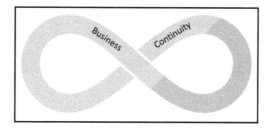

Competitive advantage is a prerequisite for continuity. CX enables companies to gather and store large amounts of customer data and analyze it. A data-driven analysis must be used to determine the current state of the strategy and the appropriate steps needed to align it with current business challenges. Data-driven processes are paramount for the **Continuity** of the strategy. If that strategy needs frequent adjustments, this means that the strategy is not plausible.

A strategy is not meant to stand still; it needs to evolve and develop while maintaining the stability of the value proposition.

Elements of a CX strategy

The basis of a CX strategy are **vision** and the **value proposition**. The strategy should be built from the ground up, with customer-centered processes and communication at its core.

The following diagram shows the elements of a CX strategy:

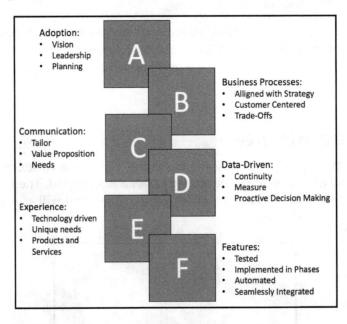

It is a prerequisite that stakeholders of the strategy are the same stakeholders that support customer-centric organization and processes. The value of the CX strategy should be measured by the value provided to customers.

Summary

It is a fact that strategy implementation is a process that can take several years and that it is a process involving a large number of company employees that depend on the success of the entire process; it shows the complexity of the variable of success or the potential failure in the details of the implementation.

In other words, we can safely conclude that the process of strategy implementation is a critical and risky process for each company. To make the process as painless as possible, it is necessary to develop a systematic approach for adjusting to new business conditions.

The categories that appear in most cases and which can be said to encompass that part of the process can be divided into four categories:

The **content of the strategy** includes the strategy design process, the consistency of the new strategy with the mission of the enterprise, and the simple and clear definition of objectives. The knowledge and experience of the people in charge of shaping the strategy in the change management process are of paramount importance.

The **strategy environment** includes the internal and external environment of the process, the internal environment that relates to the organizational structure and culture, and the management of the enterprise, because an external environment refers to the factors of the industrial and macro-environment of the enterprise.

The **operational process** includes operational planning activities, resource allocation, human resources, the communication process, and control of business activities.

The **result** evaluates the implementation process.

In the next chapter, we will discuss viable deployments, depending on the company's priorities and existing environments.

6
Organizing and Conducting an Implementation Project

The introduction of a **customer experience** (**CX**) system marks a big change to the business strategy of a company.

The implementation of a CX system covers many aspects of business enterprises, which increases the possibility of errors during deployment.

A CX system brings a new approach to the organization within a company, and companies need to ensure that their employees are ready for the new system. It is therefore important for everyone within the company to have a flexible attitude and to appreciate the benefits of a CX system.

In this chapter, we will gain an understanding of the following:

- Objectives of a CX strategy
- Planning a project
- Understanding project management methodologies
- Beginning the project planning
- Exploring implementation phases

Objectives of a CX strategy

CX is the basic strategy that integrates business processes and functions of the enterprise to create and deliver new value to customers. This is based on functional data warehouses with the support of information technology.

Understanding these objectives will help us to develop a greater understanding of the concept of CX.

The main objectives of a CX business strategy are as follows:

- **Preparing and offering services**: Services (products) are prepared according to customers' requests and wishes. The services are prepared using information collected on clients and obtained through the interaction channels.

- **Offering better customer service**: A company's profit is increased by improving relationships and identifying, attracting, and retaining the best clients.

- **A faster sales process**: CX uses sales processes that enable fast and consistent business in terms of sales and customer relationships.

- **Retaining existing customers and finding and acquiring new ones**: This creates value for the customers and thus boosts their loyalty.

- **Implementing a strategy that includes a proactive approach to the problem**: Anticipating possible problems by finding solutions before the problem occurs and creating a proactive offer of communal programs helps to save time.

Project management's inclusion in the project plan

If we look at the best project management practice (PMI methodology), then we can see that project planning involves a lot of different elements and that there is not just one project plan but several of them.

The project plan's primary design, namely project plans, includes the following:

- Integration planning, which means looking at what systems need to communicate and what they will communicate
- Planning the scope of the project (that is, what needs to be done)
- Scheduling, links between activities, duration of activities, and people accountable for realization of tasks
- Cost planning will help to determine the project's budget, and this will help monitor the costs, ensuring that the project does not exceed its budget
- Project quality planning includes looking at what quality is, who will deliver it, when, how, and with which metric
- Planning human resources, team building, and determining each team member's roles and responsibilities

- Planning team communication, management, sponsorship, reporting, and meetings
- Project-risk planning, including identifying potential risks, who is responsible for monitoring them, what comes next, how we will reduce their impact on the project, and respectively, how we will reduce the probability of dropping

- Planning how we will manage the parties concerned and how we will keep them on our side to support the project

As you can see, project planning is not a simple task, because it covers all areas of the project. Each area of the project needs to have its own plan because the successful realization of all segments of the project depends on good plans that are realistic and achievable.

It should be noted that the planning process can be repetitive. There can be many versions of a plan until a satisfactory one arises.

During the initial stages of a project, it should be mandatory to include an analysis of all the resources you use in the project, as this is important for defining the necessary activities, plan, budget, and staff, as well as other resources.

The first step of this process might be to advance the way you gather staff as well as the way in which appropriate training is to be conducted.

It is also important that the plan precisely defines the roles and responsibilities of future members of the team. Assigning responsibility to the project is of the utmost importance because it is very important to know exactly who is in charge of each activity. So, when writing a plan, you have to carefully consider everyone's responsibility and debt.

If we were to compare this process to a football match, it would be something like this: the goalkeeper, attacker, and defender should all know their respective positions and tasks. If they don't know their roles and responsibilities clearly, the team would lose their time, both in the game and in the project.

In addition to these kinds of analyses, you should consider any potential difficulties, risks, and complications that you may encounter to resolve them more successfully and over a shorter period of time.

Also consider and determine deadlines for the realization of the activities as well as the time needed for this needs to be discussed with the project team and defined in the plan.

Understanding project management methodologies

In the classifications of project management methodologies, there is a lot of confusion with regards to the methodology, framework, method, technique, or process. We will discuss two possible approaches: modern and traditional. Both of these have their own advantages and disadvantages according to the scenario in which they are used.

The traditional approach utilizes conventional tried-and-tested methods and is generally better when it comes to so-called *printing-by-numbers* projects, that is, larger projects that include clearly defined activities and phases, such as building projects or the implementation of a new operating system within the company.

The traditional approach is characterized by stricter rules (for communication, documentation, and plan changes), a greater role of the project manager, and once the project design is finished, it does not change.

By contrast, modern, agile or iterative approaches are better for the so-called R & D projects, or projects that do not clearly define the requirements. These projects are shorter. For example, the development of a new single-button communication device (iPhone), the development of a new social networking platform, or the development of a new internet platform for delivering SaaS applications.

The modern approach is characterized by less documentation, less formal communication, greater end-user engagement, smaller teams, more communication among team members, greater knowledge sharing, and participation in iteration. Too often, businesses reject some of the traditional approaches and choose modern ones, just because they are modern.

There is no wrong methodology to select for managing a project. What can become a problem is if that methodology is not a good fit for your organization.

Project management methods can be divided into the following categories:

- The traditional approach, the phased approach, or *heavy category methodology*:
    - Critical chain project management
    - Event chain methodology
    - PRINCE2

- Modern (modern project management), iterative approach, or agile project management:
    - Lean project management
    - Extreme project management
    - Benefits realization management

There is no one-solution-fits-all. You should always select a methodology that is the best fit for your company and the project.

The traditional, or phased, approach

The traditional, or phased, approach identifies a number of steps to be taken to complete the project. The traditional approach usually involves five phases:

1. The initiation phase of the project
2. The planning and development phase
3. The execution phase
4. The supervision and control phase
5. The closing phase

These phases are mostly used sequentially, but they can overlap. Different industries use different variants of these project phases. For example, in software development, this approach is known as a **waterfall model**. The waterfall pattern proved to be useful for less well-defined projects (although I do not think it is), but it is not good for larger projects that do not clearly define the functional requirements of the software.

To solve these problems, various modified waterfall methods have been published.

A traditional waterfall model

The waterfall model has been appropriated from the manufacturing and construction industry and is now used in the software industry. Both of these industries have a structured physical environment, and any subsequent changes after product delivery are virtually impossible.

During the beginning of the software-manufacturing industry, there were no formal software development methodologies, so this model was taken over.

The following is a depiction of the waterfall model:

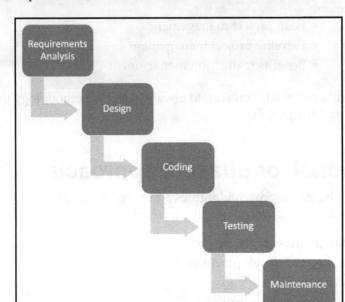

The waterfall model implies the following phases in software development:

1. Analysis of requirements
2. Development (design and programming)
3. Testing
4. Verification
5. Maintenance

Advantage of traditional waterfall model

These phases are sequential, which means that only after the completion of one phase will it pass to the second phase. Consequently, after the software goes from one phase to another, it cannot go back to the previous one.

Disadvantage of the traditional waterfall model

Since the software cannot go back to the previous phase, this is also the biggest flaw in this model, which has led to the development of modified models.

A modified waterfall model

As previously mentioned, the emergence of the modified model is a result of the drawbacks of the traditional waterfall model.

The phases are the same as seen in the traditional model, the main difference being that the phases can overlap, which gives the model flexibility. This allows for a range of tasks from different phases to be executed at the same time, further allowing bugs to be eliminated in the development phase rather than just in the implementation or maintenance phase, when the costs are huge. It also allows for changes in design during programming or testing.

Advantages of the modified model

The advantage of this model is also the reduction in the amount of documentation, which allows programmers to do more work.

Disadvantages of the modified model

The disadvantage of this model is that it is difficult to check progress because there is a possibility that at one point three or four *active* phases are possible. In addition to this, there are still some dependencies between stages that are the same as in the traditional model. These dependencies can further complicate the project with a large phase overlap, and there may be a need for the development team to go back to the previous phase to define it in detail, leading to a significant delay.

This problem can be solved by setting finite metrics for each phase. Despite these shortcomings, this model is widely used in the software-manufacturing industry.

Critical chain project management

This method was created in response to the problem of delays in a large number of projects in relation to the plan, where there were higher costs than anticipated and fewer functions than expected.

When designing a project schedule, the most commonly used methods are the **critical path method (CPM)** and the **program evaluation review technique (PERT)**. These can be used to define an activity, define the sequence of activities, and determine the duration of an activity.

When determining the duration of an individual activity, the project manager tries to secure more time than is actually needed. However, this has several shortcomings that lead to delays in projects.

Specifically, the following three problems occur:

- The task/activity is not executed until the end of its time (student syndrome)
- Tasks/activities are performed in a way that we can finish them by the deadline, although we can finish them earlier (Parkinson's Law)
- We only choose tasks that fit into the allotted time (cherry-picking tasks)

So, the security time we've engaged in performing the activity is overruled. In addition, management often forces people to perform more than one task at a time (sometimes for completely irrelevant reasons). Therefore, people jump from one task to another and extend the time provided by the plan, and by doing so, it takes them much more time to execute an activity than to perform one activity at a time.

In addition to this, people often do not want to report that the task has been completed before time because the next task is planned according to previous experience, meaning that the time scheduled for similar tasks is shortened.

Critical chain project management (**CCPM**) is trying to solve these problems as follows:

- **Critical chain**: Defines the **critical chain** (**CC**) - that is, the longest chain of dependent tasks. In this case, *dependency* refers to resources, sharing resources for the same activity, and logical activity dependence. This is the main difference compared to CPM, where only the logical dependency of the activity is considered.
- **Time activity assessments**: To reduce the time lag associated with excessive safety time, CCPM proposes a reduction in the activity time by 50%.
- **Security**: CCPM uses security buffers to manage uncertainties during project execution. The safety time that was defined for each task has now been raised to the project level. There are three types of security buffers that ensure the security of project realization:
  - **Project buffer**: This is the time added at the end between the last task and the project completion date. Any delay in the longest chain will consume some of those buffers, but the end date will remain intact. It is recommended that it be half the duration of the total safety time of all activities. Consequently, the total duration of the project is 75% of the original planned.
  - **Feeding buckets**: Delays in CC or long chains can cause project delays, as some of the critical chain vulnerabilities will be delayed. To disable them, add the feed buffers between the last task on the input path and the CC. It is recommended that they be half the time of the safety time of all the incoming route activities.

- **Resource buffer**: This can be placed next to the CC to provide enough people and skills needed for CC work.

- **Priorities**: All resources on the project are given clear and defined priorities related to maintaining CC, depending on the particular buffer, as well as information about the project in its entirety. A resource that has more than one open task before completing any task on the path that enters the CC will be assigned to that task that endangers the CC.

- **Completion**: Resources are encouraged to end the activities in the quickest possible way without compromising quality. Tasks are not left half-finished so that multitasking is avoided. Taking security time *adds* resources to what is being worked on and eliminates the previously mentioned student syndrome and Parkinson's Law.

- **Buffer management**: The amount of consumption of each buffer relative to the duration of the project tells us how many delays affect the deadline. If variations of the project are evenly distributed, then the buffer consumption will be linear. The result will be the project completed with the whole exploited buffer. If the buffer consumption is larger than the project's progress, the PM must take corrective action.

- **Remaining time**: Activities are controlled in relation to the time it takes to complete them (measured by the amount of days) and not according to percentages. This way, they control the buffers and their utilization.

Event chain methodology

Event chain methodology supplements CPM and CCPM. This is the modeling technique of insecurity and network planning that focuses on identifying event management that can affect project deadlines. This helps to mitigate the negative impact of various events on project activities and allows easy modeling of the insecurity in the network plan.

This is based on the following principles:

- **Risk occurrence**: The likelihood of the occurrence of a risk at a certain point in the execution of an individual activity
- **Event chain**: Some events may initiate another event, leading to a chain of events that can significantly affect the course of the project's execution
- **A critical event or chain of events**: The event or chain of events that have the greatest impact on the project is determined by analysis
- **Monitoring project progress through events**: Inclusion of analyses occurs in project progress reports
- **Visualizing**: Visualization of the event chain via a diagram

PRINCE2

PRINCE2 is an acronym for **PRojects IN Controlled Environments version 2 (PRINCE2)**. This was developed by the UK government and represents the standard for managing public projects in the UK. PRINCE2 was created from earlier methods under the names **PROMPTII** and **PRINCE Project Management Methods**, which were initially developed by the **Central Computer and Telecommunications Agency (CCTA)** as a UK government standard for IT.

PRINCE2 is based on seven principles, seven themes, and seven processes. The principles are continuous business justifications of the project, learning from experience, clearly defined roles and responsibilities, phased management, outsourcing, product focus, and adaptation to the project's environment.

The seven themes are as follows:

- Business case
- Organization
- Quality
- Plan
- Risk
- Change
- Progress

Principles and themes are realized through several processes. The processes upon which the preceding themes are based are as follows:

- **Starting a project (SU)**
- **Initiating a Project (IP)**
- **Managing a project (Directing a Project – DP)**
- **Stage Control (Controlling a Stage – CS)**
- **Managing Stage Boundaries (SB)**
- **Managing Product delivery (MP)**
- **Closing a Project (CP)**

The modern, or iterative, approach

The main representative of a modern approach is the so-called **agile methodology**. To understand the bases of a modern approach better, I will describe how these methodologies have emerged. In short, they were created by the need to increase project success, because a large number of projects managed in the traditional way had problems.

Research by the Standish Group CHAOS has shown that many IT projects fail to meet the projects' budgets and that they often fail to achieve the expected benefits. These problems have been confirmed by many organizations.

The US Ministry of Defense reports that 75% of software development projects have never lived up to their expectations and their development was stopped before completion.

Other scientific research has questioned the traditional methods of managing software development projects.

In 1998, Robert D Austin and Richard L Nolan studied large projects and came to the following conclusions:

- The first mistake in managing software development projects is assuming that it is possible to plan a major software development project in detail
- Another false assumption is that it is possible to shield the plan from subsequent changes
- The third mistaken assumption is that it is reasonable and possible to finalize a large project early, at the planning stage

If users cannot say what they need and want until they use it, then the planning of large IT projects is not possible. If we cannot protect ourselves from changing requests during the software development phase, then the concepts and ideas behind the traditional waterfall method are obviously unusable.

Furthermore, it can be concluded that methods based on incremental development and the prototype approach will bring significant benefits.

Agile project management

Agile project management is an iterative and incremental method for designing and building project activities in IT, technical projects, projects for producing new products or services, and very flexible projects.

The following is a flow model for the **Agile** process:

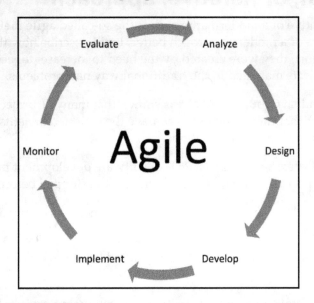

Agile works well with projects that are too complex to specify functionality before prototype testing itself. It has been developed in response to continuous and constant demands for changes during software development projects. Instead of running for weeks or months, defining the detailed specifications of the user's request for the entire project, **Agile** highlights smaller segments that can be used independently (increments), developed and tested in two- to four-week cycles.

Today, **Agile** is one of the most popular ways to manage software development projects. Agile project management was created from the Agile software development methodology and was defined by one of the signatories of Agile, Jim Highsmith. With Agile project management, the entire team is responsible for team management, not just the project leader. When it comes to processes and procedures, it is important that we use common sense and logic when writing policies and procedures. This ensures smooth running of the project, meaning that it enables faster decision-making.

In addition to being a manager, an Agile PM must display the qualities of leaders and motivators, thus raising morale during the project and maintaining discipline. An Agile PM is not the *boss* of the development team, but the coordinator of the activities and resources needed for fast and quality software development. We can say that he is an Agile PM mentor and a protector of the project team, before the manager.

Scrum

Of all the Agile methodologies, **scrum** is unique in the empirical control process. This uses the actual project progress assessment and doesn't use project performance forecasts or optimistic estimates. Scrum's projects are divided into short work cycles called **sprints**, which usually last for one, two or three weeks. At the end of each sprint, stakeholders and team members meet and evaluate the progress of the project and plan the next sprint. In this way, the direction of the project is continually relied on and determined in relation to the work done, and not on speculations and predictions.

It is not difficult to assume that this methodology is popular with project managers and developers, and it would be interesting to find out how popular a project sponsor or senior management is.

Scrum has three basic project roles, which are explained as follows:

- **Product owner**: This is the person responsible for delivering product visibility to the team and representing the customer's interest by defining product and priority requirements. This role comes with a lot of responsibility, and therefore this person has the highest authority. They are held responsible if the project fails, or if it does not meet customer expectations. The owner's biggest problem is finding the right level of involvement in the project. On the one hand, the business owner is responsible for the outcome of the project, while on the other hand, too much involvement can lower the team's independence.
- **Scrum master**: This person is the moderator between product owners and team members. They do not manage the team; they remove obstacles that prevent the team from reaching its goals. In short, the scrum master helps the team to stay creative and productive, ensures that the work is done properly, and is clear to the owner of the product at the same time.
- **Team member**: A team member is responsible for completing the job. According to some recommendations, the ideal number of team members is five to nine different experts. For example, in software projects, a typical team would consist of a developer, a designer, an analyst, a tester, a UI designer, and a database administrator. The team determines how to make a sprint, which gives them plenty of autonomy and freedom to develop, and they are also responsible for fulfilling the goals of the sprint.

Lean project management

Lean project management means applying lean concepts to project management. Lean management is a business management system with defined principles, good business practices, and tools to produce quality services and products with as little error as possible. This includes using less work, space, capital, and time. In short, this aims for production with as little waste as possible, only retaining steps that add value (namely those that the buyer is willing to pay for), those that change the product or add necessary information, and those that are legally binding or contractually binding. Accordingly, lean project management aims to create more value with as little waste as possible.

Lean was created (or, for the first time, significantly implemented) in the 1960s at the Toyota factory in Japan. This occurred in response to a specific situation (prepayment, space shortage, and an unskilled workforce) that Japanese car manufacturers found themselves in after World War II. This is known as the **Toyota Production System** (**TPS**). After the TPS principles (Toyota had 14) proved to be successful in the manufacturing industry, the system was used in other situations to improve the economy.

In *Lean Thinking,* James Womack and Daniel Jones defined five key lean principles: identify value, create a map of the value stream, create a flow, establish a pull, and search for excellence (seek perfection). If we apply them to project management, this would mean the following:

- **Identify value**: We carefully break down the project to determine which parts of the project are irrelevant and which can be eliminated.
- **Map the value stream**: We analyze the team(s) and carefully determine the course of the project to see which are needed for the project and at what time, thus optimizing the transfer of work and reducing the likelihood of creating a narrow throat.
- **Create flow**: We break the project into activities that are easier to manage. We measure performance and see how the team and individuals perform in some situations, assessing their strengths and weaknesses in order to give them the best jobs.
- **Establish pull**: Before we decide how we will achieve the activities and what results the project will produce, we will test them with project sponsors. It's better to start later and do it all at once than to start several times and keep coming back. Give the team the opportunity to make decisions, give its members more freedom to make decisions and also make them responsible for their decisions. Continuous and clear communication with team members promotes the importance of continuous learning and improvement.

Extreme project management

Extreme Project Management (**XPM**) is a method of managing complex and insecure projects. The XPM project management focus is on people, not on the methods and techniques of designing an action plan and managing the implementation of the action plan.

There are no clearly defined project phases in this approach, and there are no clear guidelines of how to realize a particular project activity. With XPM, we adapt to the project activity and we do it in the best possible way. There are no long deadlines, as they are very short, often shorter than two weeks. Team members have a great deal of freedom when it comes to deciding how to realize a particular activity, but they also bear the responsibility for deadlines and the quality of that activity. This has a remarkable impact on the human factor in this type of project management. The project's team members at XPM have completely different roles and responsibilities than they do when using traditional approaches, so the XPM project manager's main challenge is to change how the team members are thinking.

In this sense, a PM promotes the following values in changing the thinking system of the team members:

- It is normal that the demands of the project and its activities are chaotic
- Uncertainty is the only safe feature of XPM
- Such types of projects cannot be completely controlled
- Change should be accepted, not opposed
- A sense of security increases by giving team members more control

Benefits realization management

Benefits realization management is a project approach that addresses the benefits the project has for the organization in which it is realized. According to some authors, this is not part of project management, but it should certainly be highlighted as one of the new approaches to project management. It came about because many projects were declared successful, but their impact on the environment was minimal.

Under this approach, one of the PM's roles during project implementation is the project's effectiveness, not just the deadlines and results of the project. This means that during the PM project, they work closely with the project user to ensure that the product or service that the project produces is strongly embedded and accepted by the end user.

Some of the project activities that contribute to this are the following:

- Participation in presentations and demonstrations of products or services
- Workshops and training
- Preparation of marketing material
- Organizing the product launch
- Organizing and conducting meetings
- Finding causes of users' problems
- Finding creative solutions to users' problems
- Encouraging change

The benefit realization approach is the main principle—the effect comes only with change, and the change must be supported with the effect. If there is no effect, then there is no point in making any changes.

To implement the benefit realization approach, people need to change their thinking, work, and management, which is not an easy task. However, without this, the project can easily join a long list of *successful* projects whose results have never achieved the intended impact.

The main message of this approach is this: do not allow your projects to fail; consider the effects at the beginning of the project, and secure them at the end of the project.

Fit for purpose

We can conclude today that there are a large number of software management methodologies and methodologies for designing an information system.

Traditional (heavy-scale) methodologies are quite complex; they take a long time to learn and are difficult to apply, because they are quite general and require a lot of practice in their application to overcome them. By contrast, modern Agile methodologies are presented as a solution to all project management problems.

Unlike traditional methods, modern methods are very tempting because they are not too extensive, do not require much documentation, and have promising results without much learning. However, they do not yield the desired results.

It is common for everyone to adopt some derivative methodologies from the available methodologies that are more or less successful.

Let's now move on to planning the project.

Project planning

The planning of a project must be based on several questions, such as the following: what do we need to make it? How do we do what we need to do? Who will do it? When is the deadline? How much will it cost? What will it achieve?

It is interesting to note that, in most projects, planning actually begins even before you start the project itself (as one of my colleagues would say, *the project before the project*) and would not be completed even if the project itself has formally been handed over and has performed all the necessary post-mortem actions.

Each individual is responsible for each stage of the project. If your project planning is of poor quality, or you go into it with a complacent attitude, it is likely that your project will finish in the infamous 78% of projects that are started but never finished.

Delving into project planning

We can try to define project planning, but we would probably be stuck on the word *process*. Generally, the accepted definition of the planning process would be this:

- Defining work products
- Defining the quality and quantity of the work product
- Defining the resources needed

It should be observed that there is a very important difference between what is in this stage and what is contained in the stage of initiation of the project. Initiation focuses on creating and explaining the business requirements and linking the mission and goals of the organization with the pipes of the project. The project must have value to the organization that runs it and must be linked to the strategic objectives of the organization.

Planning is already one step further and focuses on concrete steps to realize the project, and answering a series of questions raised in the introduction to the chapter—or more questions, goals, and ideas that were set at the initiation stage of the project.

As you have noticed, at the stage of initiation, the cited high-level objectives of the project (still significantly related to the objectives of the organization) are these same high-level objectives elaborated on in detail. Sometimes, just a misunderstanding of the difference between the initiation and planning makes a basic error in project management—the stage of initiation is trying to describe as many elements as possible that really must be located somewhere in the planning stage of the project.

A project manager's lack of experience or a client's aggression are not good enough reasons for making non argumented changes to the project plan timeline. We have already discussed this topic in Chapter 5, *Adopting a Strategy - Organizational Changes.*

The planning process of the project

The planning process of the project differs from one methodology to the other, but almost all have common basic elements.

For the purposes of this chapter, we will define five basic elements around which we are building the planning process of the project:

- Scope
- Procurement
- Communication
- Risk
- Quality

It is interesting to note that, regardless of the approach, all the methodologies end the project-planning phase with the most accurate and concrete (correct) project plan, regardless of whether it is run on paper or uses modern project management tools.

Project reach

The planning of the project's reach is a process that ends with clearly defined elements of the project and its expectations. This should not be confused with the scope of the project document or the project initiation document. The planning of the project reach is a pre-phase of the planning process where assumptions, limitations, explanations, specifications, doubts, descriptions of work processes, and the final delivery of the project are described.

Project assumptions

Project assumptions are all of the elements of the project that need to be defined so that project delivers requirements in allotted time. For example, when setting software solutions, the assumption may be that a user has specific hardware that successfully supports a software solution.

When the construction works, the assumption is that the subcontractor has all the heavy machinery necessary to carry out their part of the deal, while the introduction of ISO standards organized according to this assumption is that the organization possesses the supporting documentation of its processes.

Note that the assumptions is not always filled at the time of writing the project's reach; it is only stated that it may be done so later during the project. Assumptions are tracked in the project plan and the risk management plan.

Project limitations

Restrictions on the project are all the elements of project planning that can affect the positive development of the project, either by slowing it down or completely stopping it. For example, when setting software solutions, the limitation may be the availability of skilled and professional workers that must participate in the project—which is often the case in our local implementations.

Restrictions on the project are not always as risky as the assumptions, and limitations are always clearly defined and easy to operate.

The explanation of the project is somewhat simpler and arises from initiating the project. Let's say that the initial part of the project explains what the strategic objectives of the project are. For example, connecting the project to the objectives of the organization, the business value that organizations can expect, the performance of the project, and so on. Here, you lack the operational and tactical levels of project objectives, and that is exactly what is defined through an explanation of the project within reach—what the targets are of the project on the operational (tactical) level. For example, project implementation software can bring increased control costs and increased profitability to the organization level, but this means making changes to the working processes of the organization that are implemented not only in software but also through changes in policies and procedures that support the current work processes.

Product specifications

The specification of the end product is always a topic on which to break the spear. The functional specification is not something that should be placed within the reach of the project, but a more detailed clarification of what is written in the initiation of the project (that is, depending on how the project began, whether as a tender or a request for a proposal) is certainly something that should be placed here.

In contrast to the specifications of the end product, the final delivery is pretty easy to define—and this is just considering what the user wants to achieve at the end of the project.

If all the conditions (objectives) of the project are met, the user will complete the project and probably confirm some sort of transfer record, which will incorporate the review of the final delivery of the project and the signatures of stakeholders.

If the conditions are satisfied, the organization at this point may not know what resources are needed for the project, what technology will be applied, and how long a project will last, but looking at the business aspect, it's quite clear what benefits the organization will receive. However, that does not mean that certain elements, such as price, duration, and performance of the project will not be listed in this document—on the contrary, these are mandatory elements of the project. But unlike individual plans that cover these items, here, they can be shown at a high level—the total price without breakdown structures, indicative of the project's duration in time/material or calendar months, and so on.

In the end, as important as it is to include all the elements that belong to the project, it is equally important to exclude those elements that the project will not cover. Why is this important? At this stage, this is perhaps not clear, but when the user deals with uncontrollable demands during the project to expand its functionality, you will remember that the *what this project does not include* list is actually your best guarantee of defense against failure of the project and business owners usually state *we thought that this implies* while providing clarity about on what exactly the project will deliver.

Finally, once you have all the elements of the project's reach, it is necessary to confirm the document. This generally refers to a formal document signed by all concerned parties of the project—users, contractors, supervisory authorities, and so on.

It is important to understand that such a signed document is the basis of the project. If anything changes in the project, it is amended to document the changes, then it causes changes to the project's parameters.

The extent of the project

When we talk about project management, most people imagine a hierarchical work breakdown structure (**WBS**)—a complete and consistent review of the tasks of the project, simply and clearly explained. Sometimes, WBS says that this is just a list of tasks considering that the main purpose of the WBS structure is to convert a large and complicated monster called the project into small, manageable units called work (project) tasks. **Project Management Body of Knowledge** (**PMBOK**) defines WBS as a *grouping of project elements that organize and define the total work scope of the project*.

Thus, it is clear that WBS is a key project element consisting of high-level user stories and descriptions, primarily geared toward management use.

The following are the basic tasks for creating a WBS structure:

- **Achieving transparent measurement of specific work activities in order to meet the objective of the project**: Although the scope of the work on a conceptual level can be defined by effort, only the WBS structure shows the exact effort needed to conduct the project.
- **Determining the required resources to perform the activities and determine the level of their knowledge and skills**: Using the WBS structure, employees receive precise instructions as they work through the project, enabling them to see where and how their work fits into the whole project.
- **Providing a basis for assessing cost and resources and the time to be engaged in the realization of the project**: Some WBS tasks must contain elements of resources, time, and effect for that task—which is the basis for the assessment of the project and the amount of resources that need to be engaged to complete the project.
- **Identifying the basis for measuring the effectiveness and actual progress of the project, depending on what the project will deliver and when the project will deliver it**: As each task in the WBS structure is simply measured (in terms of how long it takes to do it and whether it was carried out), it is easy to track the progress of the project.
- **Providing a basis for creating an effective change management in the project**: Change management addresses all changes that can occur during the project duration and how they are implemented in the project plan. Also, it establishes formal processes that document each decision and the reasoning behind it.

An overly detailed specification of tasks is probably not effective in terms of time and resources, and sometimes it really is not possible to achieve (imagine that part of the project depends on the results of product-testing in a laboratory). However, try to explain each task well.

Creating a WBS

So, how do we access the creation of the WBS structure? Although at first sight it looks a bit complicated, even the use of a pencil and paper is enough to create a fully detailed (not necessarily complex) structure task. Remember that you have to start the necessary scope of the project, which defines the basic objectives of the project and also the ways we will achieve them. Now it is up to us to define the details, which will be a painstaking task.

There are two basic approaches for creating WBS structure:

- Through the use of a formal methodology
- Through the application of the final delivery

One does not exclude the other; on the contrary, a formal methodology always contains elements of the final delivery—only the project formally leads the methodology, and an individual delivery coincides with the completion of each phase of formal methodologies. So let us see one example of creating WBS structure:

- Project:
  - On a goal of the project
  - On the project aims to B
  - On the project aims to C

When using a formal way to describe WBS, we will produce this structure:

- Project:
  - **On Project**: Initiation
  - **On Project**: Planning
  - **Project**: Execution
    - **Project Execution**: The execution of project A
    - **Project Execution**: The execution of project B
    - **Project Execution**: The execution of project C
  - On Project Control:
    - **Project Control**: The project A
    - **Project Control**: The project B
    - **Project Control**: The project C
  - On Project closing

Another way of presenting the WBS structure is shown here:

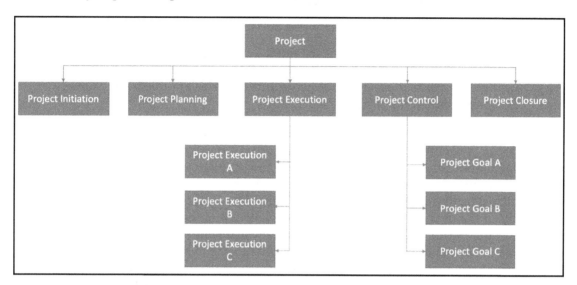

The preceding chart provides a clear picture of what is needed to be done, but it is a hierarchical list view, which is much more convenient, especially if the project consists of tens or hundreds of tasks. To update such as a WBS structure is much simpler than a graphical chart form.

To fully understand how to execute a WBS structure, it is important to note that there are two types of WBS tasks: a **collective task** and a **work task**.

A cumulative task is a collection of individual tasks which in itself does not represent one task; its execution occurs only when it has fully completed all the work.

For example, in the previous diagram, project execution is a collective task, while **Project Execution A**, **Project Execution B**, and **Project Execution C** are work tasks. Only when performing all three tasks, can we consider the collective task to be executed.

Always keep in mind what really serves the collective task: by itself, it does not have any action connected to itself; it is used for purposes of clarification and information. If the summary task does not have these qualities, feel free to delete it from the structure.

The form is largely dependent on the methodology, but it is necessary to pay attention to the forms and templates that describe the methodology.

Creating a WBS structure

There are five basic steps to be taken to build a good WBS structure.

First, start from the top of the building, then work down to the most detailed tasks. Structure is conventionally built from the top (major) to the bottom (minor). Elements (tasks) are quite similar to those used in Microsoft Word. This approach is commonly known as **top–bottom access** in scientific literature.

Typically, peak elements are precisely those elements that appear in the vision scope or charter documents of the project. Time and time again, you should ensure that management understands what you build in the project plan (using the WBS structure), because we repeat their objectives that are defined in these documents. Of course, assume that it will just be those high-level descriptive guidelines because, as has been said, the documents of that type are not going to be too detailed. Building a structure in a clear way is not easy, and the only correct way is using widely available software for project management. For example, a Microsoft project. It is hard to imagine that you will do all this correctly the first time, and there will be no change—work tasks will be moved and changed on a daily basis at the time of planning, and it's nice to have a handy piece of smart software that will make this easier.

Next, be sure to include the correct name for all of the tasks that end with a particular project delivery. Naming tasks is very simple—if you move from the delivery, then such a delivery requires the use of nouns—*hardware, software, documentation,* and so on. You also need to add verbs—*setting hardware, software installation, delivery of documents,* and so on.

The next step is to further upgrade and decompose tasks and to reapply the nomination process. Thus, for example, *installation programs* may consist of *hardware* and *software code,* or *preparing hardware, test hardware, installation program code, verification program code,* and so on. While this seems simple, it requires the involvement of all members of the project team, and as for the manager of the project, it will be difficult to know that all project tasks necessary to establish the project are successfully completed.

Usually, peak assignments can be defined by a manager or an expert, but after that subdivisions of the tasks are assigned to a team member so that all the necessary tasks are defined. Before this is done, it is imperative that the unified naming of tasks and task decomposition is adopted. It is interesting to note that this approach somehow buys the involvement of team members in the project because members of the team themselves define what they are doing and what their tasks expect them to do.

Remember to stick to the rules of 8/80. In fact, here, it is better to start with a discussion about the possible minimum or maximum duration of tasks.

I've seen tasks that last for several months and include several resources—but, then, such *mega-jobs* (wrongly called **assignments**) are more subprojects or projects themselves. These tasks are doomed from the start, not only making it virtually impossible to track their origins and the course of that certainty, but also making it impossible to obtain general information about the condition or quality of the task. Consequently, the golden rule is this: *follow the 8/80 rule.* It's very simple—none of the tasks should take fewer than eight hours, and no task should take more than 80 hours. That is to say, no more than one task should be worked on per day, and one task should not take longer than two weeks. Note that we are talking about two *working* weeks, which means 10 working days, not 14—unless your working week is defined differently.

Next, stick to the rules checkpoints. As with the previous rules, there are already control points; use these to limit the project's tasks. Checkpoints are usually defined and scheduled in advance as they are used for reporting purposes. Consequently, it is easier to report on the status of the project. Some authors say it would be nice to have weekly meetings and reports so that no task lasts longer than a week. However, that it is contrary to the 8/80 rule; it is up to you to determine whether such checkpoints have a point of reporting or a single checkpoint project (milestones). If you choose the latter, then things are clear, but because of the rules of project management, no task can last longer than the control point.

Lastly, there are other general rules for defining tasks. Other rules are not *rules* per se, but the outcome of rational decision-making by the group with regards to how to create tasks in the project. For example, the manager of the project will still have the best sense of how much detail to put into the development of the project's tasks. The manager may act as though the 8/80 rule is very intuitive and rational, but he may still want to micromanage certain tasks. Similarly, if you have problems with resources in the project, it is likely that you will adopt your own approach to a task.

Project management has been around for hundreds of years, although, of course, it has not always been known by this term. This just means that the project is similar or identical to one that has already been completed somewhere, and the question is how the project plan looks and matches your needs.

You can easily refer to the internet or another company regarding information about project management, and very soon you will have a sound project plan (or other documentation) that explains how to solve a specific task. This will also show how other people approach problem-solving. However, these templates may not always be the best solution for you.

Planning a WBS project

At a time when certain organizations successfully implement their projects, others still achieve only average results; studies suggest that average or poor results are a result of poorly planned projects.

So, how do you identify a poorly planned project? Let's see:

1. **Planning does not exist**: By far the biggest problem with planning is the lack of plans, and this is a sin that is very easy to avoid. A person does not have to be an expert to be able to plan effectively. There are countless examples in which amateur-led projects were successfully completed simply due to the fact that all the people involved in the project discussed it at great length. If you need to choose between *experts* in planning who do not go into detail regarding the plan and amateurs who will go through a project thoroughly, I would suggest that you always choose the amateurs.

2. **Insufficient attention given to specific project activities**: Some project plans are dependent on the idea that nobody in the project team will get sick, go to training, take a vacation, or simply quit. Key activities are generally underestimated—plans that are based on unrealistic assumptions are generally the worst ones. There are many variations of these. Some projects simply ignore the fact that it is necessary to create and (if for example, we take software products) set programs, convert data from old or previous versions of the program, to prepare for the transition to a new software solution, carry out detailed testing of the compatibility, and do all the other unexpected work that still exists in the project, but the majority of managers ignored this because it is was not part of the execution of the basic functionality. Sometimes, projects have been delayed because of trying to make up for lost time by reducing the time planned to test the products.

3. **Lack of risk management**: For most projects, actively avoiding errors is essential. In most business environments, the word *risk* is generally not mentioned until the project is in deep trouble. A project manager who uses the word *risk* every day but does not include risk management in his plans is probably not doing his job properly.

4. **The use of the same project plan for each project**: Some organizations develop their approaches and methodologies to manage projects, an approach known as *the way we do it here*. When organizations use this approach, any new project that is similar to the old project has a good chance of success. However, when a new project is not like the old project, the use of existing plans for the management of the project can be detrimental to the project. Good project plans always address the specific conditions in which the project grows. Most of the elements can be reused, but the project managers must carefully consider where a particular element of the previous plan can be applied in the environment of the new project.

5. **Simplified templates for project plans**: No *outside* expert can fully understand the specific needs of the project as the people who are directly involved in the project - those who create the actual project plan - must adjust the expert's plan according to the requirements of their project. Experience has shown that project managers usually have enough knowledge to choose which parts of the templates can be used in a project.

6. **The project plan is not realistic**: The usual approach to planning involves creating a project plan at the beginning of the project, which is then postponed somewhere on a shelf and collects dust during the rest of the project. As the project requirements change, the plan becomes incomplete and invalid, so that already somewhere the project purpose is lost, and there is no connection between the original and the actual project plan.

7. **An overly detailed plan too early in the project**: Some managers of projects will try to anticipate the whole project and all activities related to it as early as possible. However, most of the project consists of constantly changing the set of decisions that affect the actual running of the project—one design phase creates dependency for another project phase, and so on. So, how do managers predict the future without a crystal ball? How do they try to plan activities that are almost unpredictable and are really just an exercise in bureaucracy, which is almost as bad as the complete absence of a project plan?

The more effort that is invested in the creation of a very detailed project plan in the early stages of the project, the more likely it is that the end result of the plan will be gathering dust on a shelf somewhere (mortal sin #6). While no one likes to throw away something that has had a lot of effort invested into it, managers sometimes try to foresee the reality of the project to adjust the previously defined plans with the current case scenario. I believe that good governance projects are like driving a car with the lights on at night. The driver can have a map that will tell them how to get from city A to city B, but the driver can only ever see in advance what car lights illuminate. For the medium-sized and large projects, it is necessary to make high-level project plans affecting processes from the start to the finish of the project. Detailed, micro-level plans must be developed at the stage of planning for the next few weeks, or if the project allows for it, using the *just in time* principle of planning:

- **Planning post-completion tasks**: A typical mistake that leads to projects being delayed is planning with buffer times, to compensate for a delay later in the project. The thinking behind this is that the team struggled at the start of the project, and so we had to learn from their mistakes. However, now that we have passed that stage, we know what to do and are able to quickly complete the project—wrong! Studies show that projects rarely make up for lost time—quite the opposite. Most projects continue to waste time during the entire course of the project. This error comes down to thinking that project teams make their most important decisions relatively early in the project—the time for adopting new technologies, new business knowledge, and new methodologies.
  As teams continue to work on the project, the project is not accelerating; on the contrary, it slows down as the team deals with the consequences of incorrect decisions that were previously made, and so more time is spent correcting the consequences of these decisions.

- **Not learning from mistakes**: The greatest mortal sin that someone can commit is not to learn from the mistakes that were made. Projects can last a long time, and human memories can become less vivid over time. By the end of a long project, it will be difficult to remember all the decisions that affected the project. One of the best ways to cope with this problem and thus prevent some other mortal sins from occurring is to conduct a structured project postmortem examination. A postmortem examination may not erase the sins that were made during the project, but it will certainly help to ensure that the same ones are not repeated in future projects.

Speaking of work tasks, it is essential that you do not confuse the difference between working tasks and activities. Although some sources separate their meanings, it is better to identify them and thus inherently simplify the understanding of what the project should do. So, what exactly is an assignment? A task is a unit of work that can be performed by one or two employees, taking no more than two weeks (at least according to one of the countless definitions). Where are these guidelines commonly used? If an assignment must be performed by more than two employees, it is probably a good sign that it should be broken into subtasks.

If an assignment lasts longer than two weeks, it will likely be more complicated to keep track the current task and whether it will successfully complete. So, why the emphasis on work tasks? Well, according to the theory of planning, well-defined work tasks will not only simplify the execution of the project but will also determine which resources they need and how long the project will ultimately take. The price of resources, or the cost of the project (depending on whether you are considering the time/material or a fixed-fee cost approach) are the two main things that you will discuss with *upper* management. Or with its direct manager, depending on whether you're doing well or the project is in trouble.

Assigning work

What does a work assignment consist of? This must be the first question that arises at the start of a project. We will outline some terms of reference that are usually used to describe work; this does not mean that you should use all of them, but only the ones that you see fit:

- **Name of reference**: It may seem dumb at first glance, but the name of the reference should be well defined (that is, it must be meaningful). Do not write literary compositions.
- **Owner of the reference**: This is simpler, referring to who *owns* the project task. It is important that the owner is always just one person, no matter how many employees are assigned to the task (remember that one project's task can include more than one person, and it is recommended to have a maximum of two). Only one of them can be the owner of a project's task. But this again is relative—the owner of the project's task does not need to be part of the team that will carry out the terms of reference.

- **Number of work tasks**: There will be many people saying that this doesn't benefit the project. However, you will require some referencing here—if your project has hundreds of jobs, it will be quite hard to find a particular job when you need it. However, if the jobs are numbered, then this is easy. Most average software solutions have an automated assignment of numbers so that aspect does not need special attention. For those who prefer to use *their* tools, such as management tasks in Notepad, here is a little advice: do not assign numbers until you have completely organized *all* tasks. If you don't do this, you will have the tedious job of changing the sequence of numbers each time you change the WBS structure.

- **Starting of the work task**: This is the date of commencement of the work on the job. If you use the software, then the determination of the start of work on the job is quite a simple thing—the beginning is mainly determined by the previous work tasks (that is, their onset and the duration of the task). On the other hand, if there is parallelism or if tasks are independent of the previous tasks, then determining this at the beginning of the resource planning is an independent branch of the project.

- **The duration of the assignment**: The duration is a measure of time from the beginning of the assignment to its final execution. So, the difference between the duration and the effect of the assignment is the effect of the total time spent on the realization of the work task. For example, an employee may work only four hours a day and if the task takes 20 hours, this means that a total of five days are needed to complete the task. This is the effect of 20 hours, but the duration of the assignment is five days. A smart employer pays for the performance, and not the duration.

Who determines the duration and the effect of the assignment? Although it should be a rule that it is always determined by the employee who will carry out the task, this is not always the case. Project resources sometimes exaggerate and give very unreasonable time frames for the duration of individual tasks. For example, if a consultant provides an estimate of 10 days for a certain task, the Project Manager usually cannot assess if this estimate is accurate or not. Usually, consultants estimates include a buffers and tasks usually end as predicted in the project plan. Of course, an employee will try to make the duration of the terms of reference to be exactly as specified in the project plan. This dilemma outlines the question—who is more important, the project manager or the consultant? How much of the project does a professional project manager know about? Here, I am not talking about how the project will evolve but what the project will achieve in order to collect all this data.

To formalize tasks, we can use the following form:

Description of the work task		
Task name the owner		
of the task WBS Number		
		Resources
Start Runtime		
Performance		
Addictions		
Remarks		

You may notice some settings that have not been mentioned so far. This includes the following:

- **Addictions**: This area lists the work tasks (mostly just the WBS number) that are required to complete before the project manager can begin (or end, depending on the type of work task) the current working task. For example, before looking at testing products, you need to create test scenarios, determine the test users, create test documentation, and educate the users.
- **Notes**: Well, this is easy—here, it is possible to further describe the work task—from the name of the assignment it will be difficult to understand, and the intelligent readers (employees) have a rather thankless task, which is to forecast. So, it is better to describe in more detail what should be achieved by the actual working task. Sometimes, at work, we may need an additional category of *more*, where more notes can be added, like the beneficiaries. This will help us to learn what kind of functionality we want from the final product.
- **Resources**: A question that arises often is this: who will design the task? Sometimes, you are not able to immediately enter the exact name of the employee who will design a task, but it is possible to enter a position (for example—*software developer*), and subsequently determine the person. On the other hand, if you do not have a software tool that will help you deal with the distribution of resources, it is better to leave only one position and do not organize the staff until you have all the elements of project completion— this will be a challenge.

One of the fundamental errors made by project managers is having a lack of flexibility when it comes to a project plan. In this case, the project manager should not only be concerned about the project plan, but also the entire project structure, which includes compiling a list of tasks. In fact, everything in the project may change, including the amount of work, the duration and the scope. Here, the only question is whether it is possible to deal with changes in a controlled manner. As the project unfolds, it will change and the project will therefore proceed faster or become delayed, and we will need more or fewer resources for different tasks. This is quite normal—just take some time to consider how to deal with the changes.

So, if a change occurs (for example—the duration of the task is to increase from two to three days, which is quite wrong), consider risk management, which should address the issues of poor planning.

Poor planning arises because of a lack of information that is needed when planning tasks. What we have is less information available, bad planning of tasks, and unclear parameters with regards to the scope, time, and resources. Do we have a problem with a lack of information? This assignment should be noted as a risk in the risks table, which is an integral part of risk management (you can read more about this in the respective chapter).

Scheduling

Sometimes, the process of time management is similar to a bunch of defined tasks, estimating the duration and effect of the same and available (and unavailable) resources that you can use in your project. So, how can we achieve the realization of a project's tasks? What tasks will be carried out first and when? What tasks can be run in parallel that should take place before the start of other tasks? Answers to these and similar questions allow us to manage time effectively.

Time management effort needs a full-time business manager of the project and if the appropriate applications are not available, there is a high probability of inappropriate time management within the project.

Using these tools greatly simplifies the process for a beginner; it may seem that this is a fairly simple part of project planning.

Apart from graphically leading you through the organization of work tasks and their parallelism, duration and effect, the tool can simplify and understand the process of time management (just look at the beauty of using the Gantt Chart Project Viewer), but be careful if you do not exactly know what you are doing, as it can provide the wrong information about the duration of a particular task or of the overall project.

The aim of this chapter is not only to give you an understanding of the basic principles of how to manage time in a project, but also to point to some of the best approaches to this. This is because if there is one pervasive project management error, it is inappropriate task time management. The result of incorrect time management usually means that the projects are late, the staff are overwhelmed, and the customer is dissatisfied.

Poor planning is usually caused by a lack of crucial information that is needed for task planning. The less information we have, the lower the quality of the plan. Usually, mistakes are made in one of these parameters—the project scope, the time and the resources.

If we are lacking the information regarding a task, we need to note it as a risk in the risk table, which is an integral part of a project's risk management.

Let's discuss a scenario. After we determined exactly what needed to be done in the project by using the definition of the project tasks, we sat at the table, defined the resources we used and their effectiveness, and then we created a timetable and released it when we finished the project, so the marketing and management team could plan a party for when the project is complete.

In reality, almost no project has met such expectations. Generally, at least a few requirements or restrictions in the project are not delivered. However, the best projects will address management's ideas or desires to a satisfactory degree, which will result in successful project closure. For project to be successful it must address desires and needs outlined by project owners and management. Does that mean that the person is a professional or a consultant who - through experience or using an unfamiliar methodology—can predict when the project will end?

What is usually missing at this point are the available resources, time, detailed planning, and so on.

As previously mentioned, most projects are in crisis because of unrealistic expectations. How to solve this problem depends on the particular project, but avoiding such expectations still requires a little knowledge of planning. So, if you have quality planning, you may need someone to successfully explain how many days you need to complete the project. If you want to achieve appropriate quality in your planning, you will need inputs from subject matter experts that will provide clarity regarding the number of days and resources needed to complete the project. Once again, the radius method here is definitely not an option.

The first step in the creation of time management is to create a network diagram of tasks to be carried out during the project. As always, this will help software support, but for smaller projects or sub-projects, there is a simple manual method for doing something such as this. The principle is simple:

1. Project tasks are placed in a certain order. The first task is **Task 1**, the task that follows this is **Task 2**, and so on.
2. So, **Task 2** cannot be executed before **Task 1** is complete. This all sounds incredibly simple, but in practice, **Task 2** can start before **Task 1** has finished, and so on.

Here is a simple task flow:

The arrows between certain tasks indicate the order and the direction of the execution of certain tasks. In reality, one task may depend on multiple project tasks, and more tasks may depend on one project task.

The following is a more complex task flow:

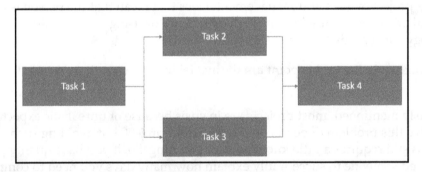

As can be seen from the following diagram, the flow of project tasks can be separated in parallel and then reconnected—it all depends on the progress of the project.

Also, the flow of tasks can be separated and continue to numerous parallel flows, each of which will have its end.

This is a parallel task flow:

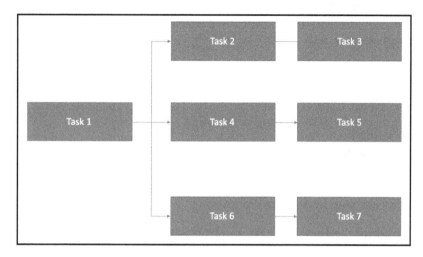

A parallel flow of unfolding tasks is always the most effective way of resolving the issue of the speed of the project. Theoretically, if they had enough resources that could project tasks, the entire project would be able to complete in one step (of course, this is only in theory, but not feasible in practice, though some tasks precede others). However, any slightly more complex project will have an abundance of parallel tasks to be joined prior, and these are required for other tasks.

The whole matrix network diagram will then be very exciting and spaciously large, but still easy to read—one of the advantages of a network diagram is the ease of the monitoring of individual flows in the project—which preceded what is necessary to do in the current project task.

So, what does this have to do with time management? When you finish the network diagram, it is necessary to take into account the duration of what is predicted for each project task. You must also set up information appropriately, add the task's duration time and calculate the total duration of the project.

Critical path

I know that there are project managers who think that a successful project needs enough time to schedule project tasks and calculate the critical path. This does not mean that managers have no idea what they are doing, but to calculate the critical path always requires significant attention—it is always possible to see one of the priority tasks of the project settings.

Critical path calculation is performed by our software solutions and hardly any project manager will engage in this. It is much easier to enter the project information into the program, which provides us with a graphical presentation of the critical path via a Pert Diagram and outlines it in red.

Critical path calculation

In simple terms, the calculation of the critical path consists of three steps:

1. Calculating the forward-pass value
2. Calculating the backward-pass value
3. Calculating the critical path

Let's understand each step in detail, as follows:

- **Calculating the forward-pass value**: This part of the calculation of the critical path is performed using two dates — the earliest possible start of the work (early start date) and the earliest possible completion of the work (early finish date). As the name says, the earliest possible start date on which - given the other circumstances of the project and depending on which task is related to the previous tasks and resources - it is possible to start work on a task. Similarly, the earliest possible completion of the work outlines the earliest possible date to finish the task, considering all other circumstances of the project and dependencies. A forward pass begins with the first task in the project and ends with the last task in the project—the earliest possible completion of the last task at the same time is the earliest possible completion of the entire project

- **Calculating the backward-pass value.** This part of the calculation of the critical path is also performed with the use of two dates, the latest possible start of work (the late start date), and the latest possible completion of the work (the late finish date). This shows the last possible start date of the task so that next task starts on time. Similarly, the latest possible completion of the work is the date when the latest task must be completed so that the next tasks start on the scheduled time. Unlike the forward pass approach, a backward pass moves to the last task in the project and returns to the beginning of the project—as would be expected, the latest possible start of the first task in the project is the latest date when the project must start to be completed in the scheduled time.

- **Calculating the critical path**: This is the calculated float (**slack**), or the time for which we can delay the onset of the task without compromising the latest possible completion of the project. Commonly, the slack is calculated as the difference between the earliest possible beginning and the latest possible beginning or the earliest possible end and the latest possible end. For example, some tasks may have a slack value greater than zero, which means that specific tasks can be delayed for so many days without compromising the latest possible completion of the project. Some tasks will have a slack value of zero; all tasks that have a value of zero make the critical path of the project.

This means that these tasks cannot be delayed even for one day. If they are delayed, then the project completion date is also delayed. Usually, the project management software automatically calculates and displays critical path, so you are always aware of the consequences that cause delays in your project plan. Also, you can get insight about which tasks can be delayed without influencing the project closure date.

PERT chart

The PERT chart is used to recognize the critical path and to find a way to shorten it.

The PERT method is a network-planning method that determines the duration (and the costs) of the project. The character of the PERT technique is probabilistic, so it is used in cases where we cannot safely say how much the duration or the cost of some project activities will be.

The PERT method was developed in 1958 at the request of the US Navy. Its research involved the collaboration of a large number of military and civilian organizations in the planning of the space program, the Polaris missile program. The method was initially called the Evaluation Research Task Program, and later changed its name to the Program Evaluation and Review Technique. The abbreviation PERT comes from **Program Evaluation and Review Technique**.

PERT technology enables project managers to do the following:

- Develop more realistic cost estimates
- Determine the total time needed to complete the project with greater accuracy
- Identify activities that depend on estimated time and/or costs

- Assess how much each activity will cost and how long it will last
- Determine the most efficient method of accelerating projects at various stages of development
- Quickly identify problems (delays or excessive costs)
- Make a new schedule of activities and the allocation of resources, if necessary

Here are the basic principles of the PERT method:

- Shorten the activities that lie on the critical path until the transfer occurs critically, that is to say, until a critical path has emerged
- If it is possible to shorten the duration of several activities, then we first need to be able to shorten the time of those activities whose costs of shortening are the smallest
- In the case of network diagrams that have more critical paths, each critical time is shortened for the same number of time units; shorten activities where doing so is most effective
- The process continues until the desired completion time is reached or at least until one critical route takes advantage of all the possible shortenings of the duration of the activity

Here is some example data in a PERT chart:

Activity	Time in days	Cost
A (1-2)	3	500
B (1-3)	4	600
C (1-4)	6	900
D (2-5)	8	300
E (3-6)	17	800
F (4-6)	3	600
G (5-6)	5	400

The PERT chart for the preceding example is as follows:

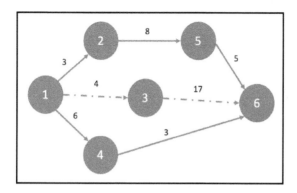

The lowest average cost of spending has activity (3, 6) on the critical path. This activity will be reduced from 17 to 12 days. The duration of the project was shortened to five days and now amounts to 16 days. After this shortening, there is a network diagram with two critical paths—(1, 3), (3, 6) and (1, 2), (2, 5), (5, 6) with the same duration of 16 days.

Due to the shortening of activity (3, 6), the costs are increased by $5 * 40,000 = 200,000$ (a hypothetical calculation). The total costs now amount to $4,100,000 + 200,000 = 4,300,000$. After this shortening, there is a network diagram with two critical paths—(1, 3), (3, 6) and (1, 2), (2, 5), (5, 6), with the same duration of 16 days:

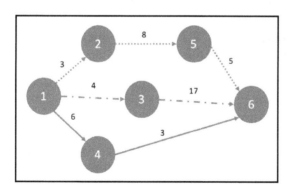

From the preceding diagram, reduction must be made on both critical times for the same number of days. From the table and the network diagram, we can see that activity (1, 3) can be shortened by three days on the critical path (1, 3), (3, 6). The same abbreviation can be obtained on the critical path (1, 2), (2, 5), (5, 6) for one day of activity (1, 2) and two days for activity (2, 5). Activity (5, 6) cannot be shortened.

At the same time, the shortening of the duration of the entire project has been completed, as there is no more activity on the critical path that could be shortened. The corresponding network diagram is as follows:

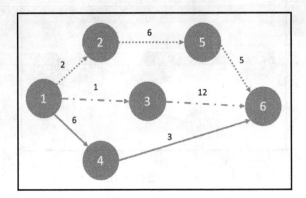

As we can see from the network diagram, we have achieved shortening the project duration from 21 to 13 days.

Implementation phases of the project

Implementing a CX system is a complex project because it requires the alignment of companies' business goals and technical constraints with the ability to integrate CX technology with existing IT systems. Consequently, management of CX implementation is important for achieving a desired result within the time frame and the planned budget.

Prior to the implementation of the CX system, the enterprise needs to make certain preparations, such as creating preconditions in order for the implementation itself to be successful. An analysis of the current state of affairs and the needs of the company is considered a prerequisite, and based on this analysis, a prepared CX business plan is required with clearly recognized requirements and goals. The company needs to predict whether the current organizational structure and computing support is a future CX solution and whether the adaptation activities are needed.

It is also necessary to identify organizational and political barriers to the launch of the CX program and, if identified, state whether they are going to be removed.

The implementation of the CX system itself follows the conceptualization and the planning of the project, which analyzes the state of the company's needs and draws up the implementation plan. The overall goal of a CX system strategy is to develop a more profitable relationship with the client.

Underlying processes

We need to understand some underlying process which help us how implementation fits in.

The underlying processes of CX development and implementation are as follows:

1. **Portfolio analysis of clients**: The primary activity of the CX chain of values is to inform clients. Collecting information to look at past client behavior and anticipating future behaviors is the basic purpose of producing a portfolio analysis. Portfolio analysis identifies current or potential consumers and classifies them into groups that are then assessed differently, and it can result in different groups of consumers being associated with different value criteria. Implement a portfolio of requirements and keep it in a regularly updated database. A well-developed database enables the company to better track customer behavior and their preferences when choosing a product/service. Based on the analysis of business performance between companies and clients, business strategies for certain consumer segments can be adapted.

2. **Customer relationship**: This is an activity aimed at identifying identity, profile, user demand analysis, and their preferences. It builds a database that has access to all employees and systems whose decisions or activities can affect the attitudes or behavior of a client. Intelligent data collection enables a good quality portfolio analysis.

3. **Network development**: To achieve CX system goals, the company must develop a network of relationships with all stakeholders in the deployment process, including partners, investors, suppliers, and employees. The market position of the company depends on the goodness of the company's connections with its stakeholders. The quality of a company's business depends not only on a company's knowledge, but on the knowledge and skills of all network members and on the joint action to achieve common goals. The precondition for the successful operation of the stakeholders in the network is the high-quality exchange of information of the network's members. In addition, the quality of products and services contributes to the success and the profit of the company.

4. **Development of a value proposition**: This is an activity where it is important to find the right ways of creating and delivering value to customers as well as sources of value creation. The customer satisfaction measurement process can help the company to understand what other customers are satisfied with and where there is a potential source of value creation.

5. **Client life cycle management**: This is a client relationship management activity. In a client life cycle management activity, attention should be paid to two sub-actions: attracting (acquiring) and retaining (retention). The company should strive to attract and retain new customers by applying the appropriate strategy. An insight into customer relationship management quality is the monitoring of retained clients so that a potential customer departure problem may have been proactively acted upon by taking corrective measures to retain clients.

Supporting processes as a precondition for successful development and implementation of CX include the following:

1. **Enterprise leadership and culture**: Enterprise management affects the outcome of the CX strategy's outcome. The management of the company makes strategic decisions which define the direction of business operations. In the case of a company with an implemented system, the operation will be directed to the client. Management seeks to respond to problems with the implementation of the CX system. If there is a marketing problem, the goal will be to improve business performance in terms of marketing activities, and if the problems in the sales process are seen as the basis for implementing CX, the goal will be expressed in terms of improving sales performance. The business mission and vision of the company will be presented.

2. **IT**: High-quality customer information is a key element of a quality CX system. IT is traced through all major CX value chain phases—portfolio analysis, customer intimacy, network development, value proposition development, and customer life cycle management. Portfolio analysis is used to identify significant and possible future users. In developing a network, IT has the task of identifying, informing, and coordinating the business network, including suppliers, partners, and employees, thereby securing their contribution to value creation. The development of the value proposition results from the collected information on the client using IT, which points to the importance of information and IT.

3. **Human resources**: This is the most important element in implementing CX's strategy for developing people's CX strategy, choosing appropriate IT solutions, creating and upgrading customer databases, creating marketing, sales and service processes, and in client conversation, contributing to customer satisfaction and their retention.

4. **Business processes**: The way businesses operate, and from a CX perspective, processes must contribute to creating value, implying efficiency (low cost) and effectiveness (delivery of desired results).

Processes are subdivided into categories in terms of scope, importance, or visibility to customers. With regard to scope, they may be as follows:

- Horizontal—multifunctional in the sense that one process involves multiple departments in its realization
- Vertical—the process is fully realized within a single business scope
- Front-office—processes that involve direct interaction with clients
- Back-office—processes that are not visible to clients

Implementation team

After understanding the underlying processes we can move ahead to see how the team works for the implementation of the project.

For the implementation of the CX system, due to its complexity, it is necessary to name a few teams that will lead the implementation process and bear full responsibility for the success of the realization. An implementation team's members represent the leadership processes. The main responsible person in the implementation team is the project implementation manager, shown as follows:

The preceding diagram shows the usual CX system implementation team in the company and consists of the following members:

- **Business Sponsor**: Responsible for establishing the company's vision and resolving potential problems that arise during the implementation
- **Project Board**: Top managers and managers of IT departments
- **Project Owner**: Manager of business functions that are most affected by the implementation of the CX system
- **Project Manager**: The person responsible for coordinating the implementation and the main person responsible for the success of the implementation of the CX system
- **Technical Lead**: The person responsible for the overall technical solution
- **Integration Expert**: The person responsible for the integration of information systems and data
- **Department Managers**: Department managers in the organizational structure of the company to which the implementation of the CX system has a direct impact in changing business processes and procedures
- **Other Members of the Project Team**: Various other experts, business analysts, knowledge experts, and so on

The project implementation of the CX system is specific to each company because each company has its own business priorities, objectives, and strategies.

Additionally, the goal for the company must be measurable in order to control the success of the process through the implementation phase and to determine whether the stated objective at the end of the implementation process has been completed.

The aim of the implementation must be attainable, relevant, and timed. It is therefore advisable that the company adopts gradual implementation of select CX functionalities. This approach prevents sudden changes in organizational culture and business processes.

All future users of the implemented system must participate in all phases of the development of CX applications to ensure that the final version of the CX system was made according to their requirements and therefore acceptance and usage of the CX system will be higher.

Summary

Planning is the foundation of everything. Successful project management involves the sublimation of several important facts. For you to accomplish your task in the best possible way and be a top project manager, you need to seriously and thoroughly plan your project, prepare a project implementation plan in advance and determine a risk assessment.

Project planning and writing project management plans is a very serious job and perhaps the toughest part of any project. You may think that the project can be successful without a well-defined and written project plan, but that is impossible. Good planning and implementation of project is highly important.

Research shows that two-thirds of the project are completed unsuccessfully, and the main reasons for this are—insufficient planning, bad communication, an inexperienced project manager, a wrongly selected project team, and the absence of the user due to their lack of involvement in the project.

If you engage with and analyze everything, you need to solve the potential problems of the project in the best way, which will make life much easier for you and your associates.

In this way, the surprise factor of the project is minimized, and you can react more quickly and better because you have already considered all the options while writing the plans. In addition to this, you will have taken preventive actions in the event that these problems are encountered.

In Chapter 7, *Scenarios and Deployments*, we will discuss possible forms of deployments, helpful tools, and the impacts of each option.

3
Section 3: Getting the Oracle CX Suite to Work as One - Advanced Settings

In this section, we will learn about the various deployment types and their impact on an organization after having identified the organizational needs.

The following chapter will be covered in this section:

- Chapter 7, *Scenarios and Deployments*

Scenarios and Deployments

7

The traditional data storage process with its on premises component has long been an inefficient way of processing data from sources generated by new technologies. The **Internet of Things** (**IoT**), big data, appliance systems, sensors, applications, and advanced devices make the processing of data and workload simple, unrepeatable, and obsolete.

The information that is displayed in organizational reports is not processed in real time and subsequently does not describe the current state of affairs. If the needs of the businesses are satisfied by applying the existing model, the previous information does not represent such an important factor.

However, most industries seek to adapt and develop their business in accordance with the time and technology available to them.

We will see how this affects our systems and learn about the following:

- Growth and technological development
- Cloud computing
- Oracle CX deployments

The rise of apps

The growth and development of technology and the global availability of the internet has brought great and rapid changes, both in the availability of information and in the way it is processed. Users now have access to real-time data. And they want to have access to information when they need it and without additional processing time.

Therefore, an effective modernized system must necessarily be adopted by the end users—but in what way?

Mobile applications or **apps** have become an integral part of end devices and sensors as they allow users to access complete and varied data. As users interact with the app, the data that is collected helps with the analysis and improvement of the user experience. The **General Data Protection Regulation (GDPR)** in this respect includes the protection of sensitive and private user data and the data that users agree to share, enabling analysis and insight and the formation of useful information for further interaction.

A look at the reality that technology and its progress brings is that it directs end-users' and information systems into the cloud-based space.

Therefore, the very concept of integrating the same uses of cloud technologies becomes one of the logical choices in the implementation of modern systems where the business of a company is key based.

Understanding cloud computing

Cloud computing is a form of network computing which provides the possibility of on-demand services. Network computing refers to a set of computers or devices from different locations connected together to share resources. When this network is taken *off-premises*, that is, to the cloud, it becomes cloud computing.

A business may choose to implement network computing over cloud computing depending on their needs. However, the problem with network computing is that if one part of the software in the node fails to perform its work, other parts on other nodes may fail too.

While this problem can be mitigated if that component has a restore point on another node, problems can still crop up if the components rely on other parts of the software to accomplish one or more network computing tasks.

This problem can be mitigated by using cloud computing since all of the resources are internally replicated. The larger the portion of the company's workload that is cloud based, the fewer resources and less expertise the company would need to maintain and run it. Thus, business continuity is assured.

Main characteristics of cloud computing

Cloud computing brings a lot of benefits that contribute to IT's economy. Some of the most important benefits can be described as follows:

- **Small start-up costs:** Most cloud-based services are pay-per-use. The services available are considered as rental equipment that are paid for depending on how much equipment is needed, at what time, and with what services it is leased. This *renting* of infrastructure allows organizations to keep their IT costs low and capital investment virtually zero.
- **More effective use of resources**: System administrators are mostly concerned about the procurement of hardware. Using cloud-computing architecture allows better and more efficient management of resources, as system admins can access applications only when they are needed and can then stop using them.
- **Reducing execution time and response time**: Applications that use clouds to perform many different cloud-computing tasks allow them to run on a variety of different servers. For example, performance can be enabled on 1,000 servers and thus speed up the workload.
  Processing in this way can be done in one-thousandth of the time that would be needed by one server.

It is important to note that cloud-computing servers are often (but not always) used together with virtualization technologies. Organizations using information technologies understand that virtualization enables them to swiftly and easily copy the existing environments, sometimes including multiple virtual machines to support the testing, development, and storage of activities.

The possibilities that cloud computing can offer to users can be quick and elastic initiated, in some cases, and automatic, in order to, if necessary, proportionally increase or decrease opportunities when they are no longer needed.

Systems that use cloud computing are automatically checked and optimized for the use of resources.
The use of resources is optimized by the impact on measurement capability abstractions appropriate to the required type of service (for example, data storage, bandwidth, or active accounts).

Also, the use of resources can also be monitored and verified. Reports can be run by providing a transparent insight to service providers' users.

For **software as a service** (**SaaS**), the service provider allocates, configures, maintains, and updates software applications on the cloud structure so that the services are equipped as expected.

For **platform as a service** (**PaaS**), the service provider manages the platform infrastructure and the cloud software used for platform components, such as databases.

So from this, we can conclude that the PaaS service provider usually develops, implements, and manages PaaS types of clouds. The IaaS service provider has control over physical hardware, and with the cloud software that makes the services of this infrastructure possible, such as physical servers, network equipment, or storage devices. Therefore, from the activities of the provider, we can describe the service as development, management, security, and privacy of clouds.

Let's understand each in detail.

SaaS

Maybe we are not even aware of it, but most people actively, in everyday life, already use at least some SaaS services. SaaS services are the simplest of the applications that users access via the internet.

SaaS can be defined as a software that is used via the internet. The software provider licenses the application to clients either as pay by use or a subscription service.

As in other cloud-computing models, it's important to ensure that the solution that is supplied by the software model as a service is in accordance with generally accepted definitions and characteristics of computing in the cloud.

Some of the more important characteristics are as follows:

- Access to commercial software is enabled via the web
- The software is operated from a central location
- The software is delivered according to the model one by one
- Users do not have to worry about software upgrades and adjustments

The **Application Program Interface** (**API**) enables the integration of different software segments (modules). One of the concrete examples of software delivery as a service is the company's software.

Along with this example, a number of others can also be listed such as email applications, financial applications, customer service applications, cost management applications, and time management applications.

SaaS may be the most famous delivery model today using computing in the cloud, but there are more examples that application creators focus on using the platform delivery model as a service.

PaaS

Just as SaaS brings significant benefits to end users, similarly, the PaaS helps creators of software applications.

PaaS can be defined as a computer platform that enables the rapid and easy development of web applications without the need to buy and maintain software and supporting infrastructure. This model is very similar to SaaS, but the difference is that there is no delivered software application here via the web, but a whole platform on which new applications can be made.

There are many important features of the platforms that are delivered as a service, but among the basic ones, are the following:

- PaaS combines development, testing, application, hosting, and application maintenance in an integrated environment. These can be all the different services needed to achieve the overall application development process.
- Web-based user-interface tools help in creating, modifying, testing, and applying different scenarios for the appearance and application of the user interface.
- The multi-tenant architecture allows multiple users simultaneous use of the same development application.
- Built expandability or scalability of used software enables the balance of hardware loading and restoration of all activities after the system has crashed.
- Integration with web services and databases with the application of general standards is enabled.
- PaaS provides full support for collaboration within and between development teams. Some platform versions include project-planning tools and communication/chat tools.

PaaS, which in many ways is similar to IaaS, still differs from it by offering certain additional services, usually available in two different ways:

- As a collaborative software development platform, it focuses on managing process flows (process workflow) regardless of the data sources used by the application
- As a platform that allows the creation of software using data owned by an application, this type of PaaS can be understood as a method of creating applications for common types or forms of data

PaaS is particularly useful in situations where a large number of creators, designers, and developers are working on the same development project or when external entities should also interact with the development process. This model is shown to be useful to those who have an existing data source; for example, sales information is derived from a customer relationship management system and the company wants to consume that data with the purpose of developing a specific application.

PaaS is also useful when the creators of an application want to automate the processes of its testing and implementation.

There are also situations in which PaaS does not, however, prove to be an ideal solution.

Here are a few examples of such situations:

- The application is highly portable.
- Non-standard languages are used to program the application or particular application-specific approaches to application development have a decisive impact on the development process and its performance.
- Non-standard languages used to program the application will make it difficult or even impossible to later transfer an application to a different environment—for example, on the computer of another manufacturer. There is also the problem of relying too much on one PaaS.
- Due to the effectiveness of the applications, the hardware and/or software adaptation to which these applications are based should be adapted.

IaaS

Infrastructure as a service (IaaS) is a way of delivering cloud-computing infrastructure. These can be server computers, data-storage spaces, networks, and operating systems.

Instead of buying computers, software, storage devices, space for hardware, and network equipment, users rent a service according to their needs and requirements.

Infrastructure delivered as a service can be implemented in several different ways—as a public or private cloud.

Just like the two previous models, the IaaS has quickly became popular.

Some features of this model are common to all of its implementation modes, which are as follows:

- All resources are distributed or delivered as services
- Dynamic extension or scaled service is enabled
- The costs of its use are variable because the payment model is applied according to usage
- The model allows the same hardware to use multiple users simultaneously

It makes sense to use IaaS in a number of situations, and the reason is the benefits that cloud computing can bring.

Situations that are particularly suitable for the implementation of IaaS are as follows:

- The demand for computer resources fluctuates a lot; over time, there is a high demand, occasionally peak loads of infrastructure can occur, while in some other periods demand for them almost disappears
- Brand-new companies (start-ups) that do not have enough capital to invest in hardware
- When an organization develops rapidly, hardware extensions and upgrades are also moving at a higher rate
- When there is growing pressure on the company's management to reduce capital expenditures and cost policy, it directs to operating expenditure
- When the needs for expanding the infrastructure that are expressed by individual parts of the organization outweigh such needs considered from the standpoint of the entire organization

However, IaaS is not appropriate or is not the right solution in quite a few instances, which are as follows:

- When the reasons for the compliance and respect of legal regulations do not speak in favor of renting stored data or leaving the processing of sensitive data to another organization
- When an extremely high level of efficiency of computer infrastructure is required, and its own infrastructure can meet such requirements

Risks in cloud computing

Because of its size and significance, the cloud-computing environment is often a target of malware, brute force, and other attacks. It is important to ask your service provider about access controls, practices to assess vulnerability, and patch management controls and configuration. This is to see whether they can sufficiently protect the system and personal information.

Sharing important data with a cloud computing service provider involves the transfer of a significant amount of organizational controls over data security to the service provider. It is therefore important that the service provider understands the needs of the organization's privacy and security.

It is also important that the service provider is familiar with the rules on the security and privacy of data that are applied under its own jurisdiction.

The prime risk involved in business continuity is the loss of internet connectivity in the cloud-computing environment. It is important to ask service providers who are in charge of securing an internet connection. You need to have a back-up plan while the service is unavailable. If a vulnerability is identified, all access to the service provider must be terminated until the vulnerability is resolved.

Many organizations are not aware of where data is located and where is it being processed, which leads to difficult data management.

User models

All three delivery models described in the previous subsection, SaaS, PaaS, and IaaS can be an integral part of any computer cloud.

However, access to these services depends on the cloud model in terms of the type or type of its application.

So, let's understand each here in the following sections.

Public cloud

The **Public Cloud** consists of computer resources that are available to users on the basis of a subscription. The following is a very generic depiction of a public cloud:

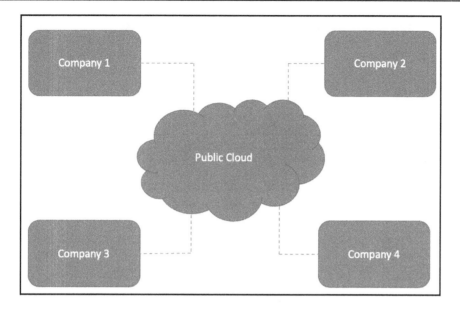

Virtualization is one of the fundamental characteristics and driving forces of the public cloud. Virtual resources in a public cloud appear and are similar to physical resources in an old computing center, but their activation, looking from the user's perspective, is much simpler—there is no need to configure resources, access to the requested resources is facilitated, and there is no administration.

Due to virtualization, these resources are not visible to the user.

A public cloud is a divisible, multi-use infrastructure on which the user uses a **service-level agreement** (**SLA**) with the service provider specifying the rights and obligations of both parties when using cloud resources.

Once subscribed and signed to a service-level agreement, the user can start using cloud resources on demand, for when and how long they want, and payment of the service is based on how much they consume. Public cloud service users are diverse. They can be individuals or small, medium, and large enterprises.

Computer resources are almost unlimited in capacity and do not require any capital investments from the users.

The resources are completely flexible, which means that the user can create, activate, and consume resources according to their own needs and without any limitations.

Regarding service users, four basic scenarios of a public cloud can be distinguished as follows:

- **Scenario 1**: By end user
- **Scenario 2**: By company
- **Scenario 3**: By end user
- **Scenario 4**: By another company

Let us understand each one by one:

- **Scenario 1**: In this scenario, the end users access the data or applications in the cloud. The most commonly used applications of this type are emails and social networking applications. The user does not need or want to know anything other than their username and password. Data is stored and managed by the cloud operator. The user is not aware of how the cloud works—if it can access the internet, it can access their data or the application they selected:

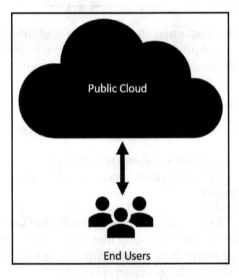

- **Scenario 2**: In this scenario, the company requires open cloud services for the needs of its internal data-processing and business processes. This scenario will be applied by companies that do not have much experience with the use of public cloud services because it allows them to establish a very high degree of control. Examples of using this scenario are the following:
    - Using the cloud storage space for storing backups of your data or storing rarely used archive data
    - Using **virtual machines** (**VM**) in the cloud when processing data, which the company carries out itself, comes to the peak load
    - Using cloud-based applications to support specific functions in a company (customer relationship management, creating event calendars, email, and so on)
    - Using a cloud database to process enterprise applications, which can be very useful when databases are shared with business partners, state administration bodies, and so on

The following diagram illustrates this:

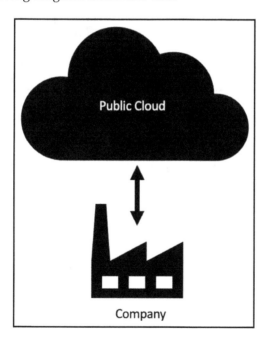

- **Scenario 3**: In this scenario, the organization uses public cloud services to provide its services to their end users. When one end user interacts with an organization, it accesses the cloud to capture data and/or processes them in order to deliver the results to another end user. The end user may be an employee or an external client of an organization:

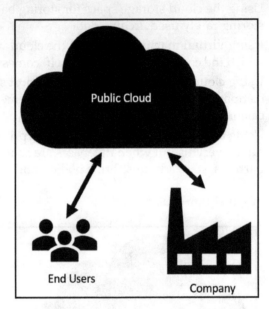

- **Scenario 4**: This scenario refers to a situation where two companies use the same public cloud. In this case, the emphasis is placed on the application of both companies, which will enable their interoperability (cooperation and interaction). This public cloud application scenario is most often used to manage the supply chain or value networks:

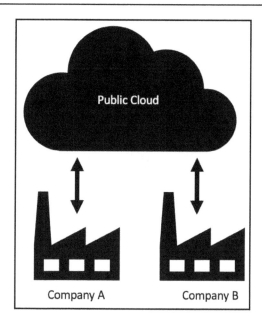

All of these four scenarios outline the use cases of the **Public Cloud**.

For companies that would like not to share their resources, then a private cloud, discussed in the next section, is a better solution.

Private cloud

The ability to provide a fairly inexpensive, convenient, and flexible approach to data, stems from the implementation of cloud computing in an organization in the form of a private or internal cloud.

In a **Private Cloud**, there is control over the entire infrastructure, data, and data-processing processes in the hands of the organization. Usually, a private cloud is implemented in the organization's accounting center, and its employees (administrators) manage it.

A private cloud maintains all of the company's data resources, such as financial records or customer data. This eliminates many security and legal issues that are inevitable when the organization's data resources are entrusted to a third party, that is, the owner or operator of the public cloud for storage, processing, and management.

In this diagram, we see that all of the workload is conducted in the cloud environment:

Virtualized infrastructure ensures the necessary level of abstraction, which allows the application or business service to be directly linked to the hardware infrastructure of server computers, data storage devices, and networks. This enables business services to freely and dynamically move among virtualized infrastructure resources in a very effective way, in accordance with predefined policies that ensure the achievement of service quality objectives.

The layer of security and identity management must include an infrastructure that will enable identity management and the implementation of a single security policy across the entire cloud, while ensuring a satisfactorily high degree of flexibility.

The development layer should include new-generation development tools that will ensure even better use of cloud-based capabilities. Such tools can not only facilitate the alignment or the orchestration of services in order to better match the current state of demand for them, but should also encourage the implementation of those business processes that can take advantage of the parallel processing data that cloud computing provides.

The use of a **Private Cloud** has fairly high operational costs. Therefore, they will mainly be used by large organizations in order to take advantage of the economies stemming from the provision of services to a large number of internal users.

Large organizations usually already have large computing centers based on some older technologies whose operating costs can be significantly reduced by the introduction of a private cloud.

Hybrid deployment

A hybrid cloud model is a model in which several clouds, public and/or private, work together. This means that one cloud service provider offers the use of its own services and resources in combination with the resources of some other service providers.

Hybrid cloud services can also be offered by an intermediary who does not have any resources in their possession, but only allows or facilitates users to use the resources of other service providers. In this case, the provider must manage a hybrid cloud over the conditions set by the user.

In this diagram, we see that workload is spread across cloud and on premises resources:

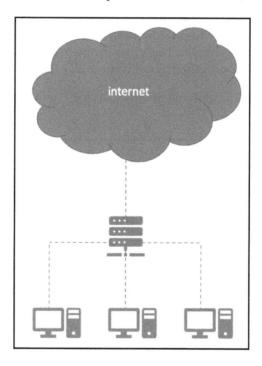

The position of users of hybrid cloud services is identical to the one in which the public cloud is used. The user of the hybrid cloud does not need to possess all of the expertise and knowledge required for its management; that is the task of the hybrid cloud service provider.

The obligations of the providers of the hybrid cloud services are equal to the obligations of the providers of public cloud services, but it is important that the SLA signed by the provider and user of the hybrid cloud service must be in some digital form and certified with a digital signature. This will enable the service provider to select the required resources in accordance with the user conditions without the need for direct employee intervention.

Managed cloud

Cloud cover can be considered as a subset of technologies and tools used in a hybrid cloud, but on the other hand, it can also be considered as a super session in relation to the private cloud model. It will be used by partner companies and privileged individuals who share some common goals, interests, or resources, and will be allowed to access private cloud services from a company if it exists, and services of one or more public clouds that all together make up a hybrid cloud in the cloud community function.

This application of the cloud model will result in savings, as costs are shared among the organizations that use them:

There are two models of community cloud usage:

- A model in which businesses and individuals approach hybrid clouds, with individuals first accessing the IT resources of their preferred users and then hybrid clouds
- A model in which a company has its own private cloud through which both itself and its authorized or privileged users access public clouds that form a hybrid cloud

Examples of community cloud applications were rare until the **New York Stock Exchange** (**NYSE**) announced the launch of its cloud community.

The purpose of that cloud was to increase the level of service to companies and individuals doing business with or through this stock exchange and to give them a level playing field.

By creating community clouds, all stock exchanges were enabled to place their virtual machines on the same infrastructure as the stock exchange servers, which provided them with the same position in the competition, and the stock market had complete control over their dealings. This example is instructive because it has strongly stimulated further development of community cloud technology. It also has demonstrated that such technology should only be used in idealized cases of extremely honest partnerships, high levels of trust, and loyalty of community members.

IT infrastructure completely ignores the computer stack below the operating system, and with the use of other models of service provision according to the SaaS model, this interaction becomes completely unnecessary.

By contrast, in the classic **Information and communication technology** (**ICT**) user infrastructure, the user is not a service user but actively participates in the management and support of information services of their own organization, which is not its core business.

It's good to notice that a user can install a shared client platform on their own infrastructure, which is much more complicated in the public cloud due to specific licensed policies of the system's supporters. For the same reason, at the highest level of the computer hack, there are options for processing all or only server applications.

Cloud bursting

Burst cloud is a model for developing applications in which the application is running in the private cloud or data center and is sprayed into the public cloud when more resources are needed to handle peak-time workloads. By using such a hybrid model, organizations pay additional resources only when they need it. Cloud bursting is usually used for high-performance applications and for non-critical applications handling insensitive data workloads. The workload is kept local and then pushed into the cloud to match peak-scale demands, or the application can be moved to the public cloud, freeing the local resources for business-critical applications.

Burst cloud is best used for applications that do not depend on a complex infrastructure delivery applications or integration with other applications, components, and interior systems of the data center.

As everything, this too has some benefits and some setbacks. Let us study both to understand about cloud bursting better.

The advantages of using bursting clouds are as follows:

- The ability to expand and pull services that are based on changes in capacity requirements
- Cost reduction, as organizations only pay for additional resources at their own request
- Increased performance, with spikes in larger loads
- Spraying of new instances of the second application cloud
- The ability to burst the application of scalable layers to improve performance in the peak periods
- Reduced cost of capital

Here are the disadvantages of using a bursting cloud:

- Problems with security, compliance, and privacy regarding moving data between environments, or other constraints or requirements involved in migrating data and/or services into a public cloud
- A public cloud must be able to meet the capacity required by private clouds and should be able to effectively maintain the balance of your workload, so as not to deteriorate when it comes to the existing services

- Delay challenges—moving the entire application to a specific location in the cloud infrastructure helps to reduce delays in the case of high-intensity workload peaks
- Clouds, if they use a public cloud within the application of a hybrid cloud, must be interoperable and have to use the same platforms to avoid inconsistencies between the different environments

Cloud bursting can help an organization to handle workload peaks without the need for a capital investment in an on premise data center.

Security aspects

The security of computing in the cloud is very important in the application of cloud computing. The application of any technology can never be perfected until there is no security problem. There is no such solution that guarantees absolute security. When companies migrate their existing cloud applications or cloud upgrades, they need to have a detailed security model that will help them develop, prevent errors, and preserve the value they invested. The biggest difference after switching to cloud computing in terms of security aspects is that the company loses control over resources it had when its applications were maintained by the company. While the resources were under the company's influence, controlling access to sensitive information and business applications was a big challenge. After the cloud transition, access control remains important, but the security infrastructure, platform, and applications are under the direct control of the cloud service provider.

Here are three aspects of cloud computing security, which, from the standpoint of organizations, show that they are very important:

- **Legal regulation**: Laws and other legal acts define security requirements as a higher priority than functional and technical requirements.
- **Security controls**: It is very important for all users to have specific security controls run by the service provider, but there are few cloud computing providers offering infrastructure that can support them all.
- **Connectivity (federalization) of security services**: In order to implement all the necessary controls, cloud service providers will often have to connect to specialized security service providers and create the conditions in which all of them will act as one. Under such conditions, it is extremely important that these services comply with generally accepted security standards that will ensure their compatibility.

Legal regulations

For various reasons, in many countries and regions of the world, the authorities in one way or another express their reservations as well as concerns about the increasingly intense and extensive use of cloud computing in the zones of their influence.

Many countries have adopted 30 very strict and restrictive privacy regulations that prohibit the storage of certain data on physical media and devices located outside that country. Organizations and the people within them have been severely punished for violating such laws. Any organization that stores sensitive cloud data must be able to prove that their cloud computing provider does not store such data on physical servers outside a particular geographic area. For example, if data is stored somewhere in Europe, a cloud computing provider from the United States will need to know European regulations that in some cases are quite different than the US ones in order to avoid problems in Europe and the US.

In addition, many professional associations, business associations, and interest groups develop their own regulations that do not have legal force but nevertheless have great influence within such a community. Examples include regulations in the areas of financial services and banking, the issuance and use of payment cards, health care, the pharmaceutical industry, air and maritime transport, and so on. Such regulations usually stem from best practices and become mandatory for members and members of the particular association.

All these real-world events are mapped into the virtual world of a computer cloud. For example, if a virtual machine is activated in a cloud, can an application processing on that machine access sensitive data? It is the so-called **gray zone** that many experts have recognized, but legislative institutions are currently far from concerning that practice, but it is almost certain that appropriate regulations will soon appear in that area. New laws can result in heavy costs for organizations that use cloud computing, because new provisions need to be implemented, and this will certainly require the introduction of certain changes to current existing practices.

Security controls

There are a lot of security controls that must be implemented in every IT environment and the information system, as well as in the application computing in the cloud. Necessary security controls today will be largely standardized.

Ten standardized security controls are described here that must be implemented in practical cloud computing realization.

Important security controls in cloud computing implementations that need to be implemented are as follows:

- **Property management**: You must be able to manage your hardware, network, and software assets (physical or virtual) that form the cloud infrastructure. This means that for the purpose of auditing and checking regulatory compliance, it must be possible to determine any physical or network access to each of the elements of that property.

- **Cryptography (key management and certificates)**: Each secure system requires an infrastructure to implement and manage cryptographic keys and certificates. This means the implementation of cryptographic functions and services based on standards for support of information security at rest and on the move. One of these is the **Key Management Interoperability Protocol** (**KMIP**).

- **Data security and storage devices**: Data encryption must be stored in order to provide data. Some users of the service will require and store their data separate from the data of other users. This control is implemented using the *IEEE P1619* standard.

- **Endpoint security**: Cloud users must be able to provide endpoint access to their cloud resources, which means they should be able to apply limitations to endpoints according to network protocols and device type.

- **Audit and event reporting**: Cloud users must be able to access cloud-based events, particularly system failures and security breaches. Cloud service providers will lose their reputation if they fail to inform the user on time about the events that occurred.

- **Identity, roles, access control, and attributes**: It must be achievable to define the identity, roles, privileges, and other attributes of individuals and services in order to implement access controls and security policies properly. To implement this control, the **Security Assertion Markup Language** (**SAML**) standard and the *X.509* certificate are used.

- **Network security**: It will be realizable to secure network traffic on the switch and router on the data packet level. Therefore, all IP protocols must be secure.

- **Security policies**: It must be possible to define and apply policies that will support access control, allocation of resources, and other decisions. Policy definition needs to be strong enough to ensure that the provisions of the SLA and licensing agreements can be implemented automatically. For this security control, the standard **eXtensible Access Control Markup Language** (**XACML**) is used.

- **Automated services**: An automated way of managing and analyzing security control flows and processes must be ensured in order to be able to conduct a safety audit and compliance. This pertains to reporting any events that violate security policies and licensing agreements made with clients.
- **Workload and service management**: There should be the potential to configure, use, and monitor the service as per defined security policies and licensing agreements with clients. For this control, the standard **Service Provisioning Markup Language** (SPML) is used.

Federalization of security services

Federalization implies the possibility of a greater number of independent resources to act as one single, unique resource. Computerization itself is an example of the federalization of resources in which many elements, identities, and configurations in cloud computing must be federalized in order to make this kind of computing practically usable.

Security requirements can be implemented using federalization in the following forms:

- **Trust**: The ability of the two parties to define a relationship of trust with some authentication authority. Federalized trust is the foundation on which all further forms of federalization can be built.
- **Identity management**: The capability for identifying a provider that accepts all user's digital credentials (user identifiers, passwords, and certificates) and returns a signed message or a token that identifies that user. Cloud service providers believe the identity provider and will use this token to allow the user to access the resources for which they are authorized, even when the cloud service provider does not know who the user actually is.
- **Access management**: The ability to generate policies that check tokens in managing access to cloud resources. This can be controlled with the help of more than one factor. So, for example, access to a resource can be restricted to users in a specific role, but only with the application of certain protocols and at a specific time.
- **Single sign-in and logout**: The ability to federalize a single application for the use of cloud services allows the user to sign in to use one application, and then access other applications that trust the same authentication authority. The federation of single sign-outs is similar because, in some situations, it will be important for the user to remove all applications that can be used simultaneously by checking off the use of one application.

- **Audit and compliance**: Audits are required to make sure this is being done with document compliance and with the provisions of the SLA and regulatory requirements.
- **Configuration management**: This is the ability to federalize the data needed for service configuration, applications, and virtual machines.

Examples of the use of cloud computing in business

In this section, we will discuss usual use cases for cloud computing in business environments and the reasoning behind them. This will be general and technology-agnostic examples. Let us understand each.

Email archiving

Email is the most widespread, and probably the most important, application used in the business. Today, it is almost impossible to imagine how any organization could function without the use of email. Managing an email system is often very complex if it is done in your territory.

Cloud computing technology is very well accepted in the case of such applications, especially as standard cloud services offer elementary security measures for email systems such as antivirus protection, spam filtering, and the continuity of electronic mail.

Many organizations, for their own or regulatory reasons, also opt for archiving electronic mail, which is a much more complex task.

Many organizations, even before the onslaught of cloud computing, were forced to invest significant resources in storage devices and storage media for the purpose of archiving electronic mail, and ever since, demand for them is constantly rising. It is an endless circle of hardware and software where purchases are closing, with a proportionate increase in investment costs and the cost of their maintenance, and also the additional cost of space for equipment and media storage.

Offers of email archiving services in the cloud include a wide range of options, increased transparency, and simpler control of compliance with legal regulations. However, many IT departments and services in organizations that have an email system in their possession find the idea of moving their archives into the cloud considerably problematic, mostly due to difficulties in migrating data, a potential loss of control over the system and trust in an outside partner that will treat them at least as carefully and securely as their owners did. Therefore, before deciding on the transition to archiving email in the cloud, a serious in-depth analysis should be carried out to determine whether it can meet all the requirements of the potential user.

Contact center

A contact center for many organizations operating over the internet is the heart of their business. As the name implies, through the contact center, contacts with existing and potential users are realized, whose information, trust, and satisfaction can be the main influence on the success of the company's business.

The establishment and operation of a contact center is usually expensive and demanding, so many companies do not use them in a sufficiently efficient way.

In order to solve this problem, companies should do the following:

- Quickly establish and deploy a contact center
- Reduce the initial and ongoing costs of the contact center
- Ensure there are rapid contact center change adjustments
- Enable flexibility in the work of the contact center staff—quickly respond to increased demand in contact center, by enabling increased number of users
- Ensure the continuity of the contact center—increase the level of customer service quality

In order to achieve these goals, the use of cloud computing for a contact center can greatly help with its services. There are many benefits that an organization can accomplish using such services, and some of them are as follows:

- **Much quicker activation of a new contact center**: The establishment of a contact center in large organizations will take up to six months and millions in budget amounts to enable it to work, and using a cloud computing service to establish a contact center can be done within a few weeks. The equipment already exists and all preparatory actions for its activation have been carried out.

- **Reduced capital costs**: Capital costs practically do not exist when starting a contact center in the cloud. The company should not buy any additional hardware or software. All that is needed is an existing telephone center and a certain number of computers with connections to the internet, and the organization pays only as much as it benefits.

- **Reduced running management costs**: The hardware and software of traditional contact centers require a lot of care and maintenance, as the rooms are full of server computers, a network, and communications equipment, and maintenance performed by qualified technicians. Excessive cloud computing need not be done anymore, and this reduces current management costs.

- **The latest technology**: Cloud computing services providers are usually in the pipeline with the latest technologies to make them more competitive on the market.

- **Better choice, retention, and flexibility in the work of the agents**: Contact center in the cloud allows simple implementation of flexible home-based work strategies. Such flexibility facilitates the recruitment and selection of quality agents and their retention in the organization. Since the highest cost of a contact center is employee salaries and office expenses, opening opportunities for work from home can reduce these costs.

- **Disadvantages as an advantage**: Disadvantages of various types can greatly disrupt the regular operations of the company, as well as its contact center. By virtualizing the contact center and moving it to the cloud, such dangers can be avoided. During various disasters, clients will receive the service of the usual quality, as it is all in the cloud.

- **Faster resolution of misunderstandings**: In the day-to-day work of a contact center, it is common to occasionally have misunderstandings and even confrontations with clients. Sometimes, it is necessary to prove who is right by analyzing the conversation being conducted between the agent and the client. The only solution to this problem is the recording of a conversation. Recording a conversation is often expensive for the organization, but the provider of a call center service in the cloud provides such a service as standard.

Customer relationship management

Customer relationship management (CRM/CX) also seeks to maximize the benefits of cloud computing. A new generation of customer relationship management services fully relies on cloud computing, using interfaces that are open to integration with other related or complementary services, such as collaborative services, information management services, network services, and information. The goal is to deliver simple and useful technology that supports human interaction with end users, which can be easily managed with the help of information technology and with which lasting business value can be achieved. Be it delivered as regular cloud services or in a hybrid combination of cloud services and services provided, customer relationship management applications can achieve collaborative effects, which will benefit both the organization and its clients.

They can also be used immediately after they are ordered or called up to allow users quick access to innovations and react to current events. The cloud service delivery model provides the ability to use almost unlimited capacity to expand or reduce the amount of resources needed, so that the organization that consumes them pays only what it uses, without any additional costs.

In addition to applications, cloud computing also offers platforms and infrastructures that are offered as services. They bring many positive effects, such as the increased productivity of employees, the establishment of better and stronger relationships with clients, and thus a higher level of customer satisfaction and their loyalty to the company.

Managing customer relationships encompasses the business processes of the company with its clients, regardless of the specifics of the activities and businesses that the company is dealing with. These deals are sales, marketing, and services provided to clients, and they are done mainly through a contact center. Generally, all applications that automate such processes serve to manage the entire life cycle of a client, including the conversion of potential into actual clients of the company and help the organization in building and maintaining successful relationships with clients.

There are two generations of CRM applications in the cloud:

- The first generation of CRM applications based on the application of cloud computing has made it possible to separate and grow the independence of the applications themselves from the delivery model, meaning that it no longer matters where the CRM applications are. It is important that they are available to employees of organizations and their clients when they need them.
- In the second generation of CRM cloud applications, the emphasis is on the benefits that cloud architecture can provide for improving the quality of an organization's relationship with clients, and these advantages are many.

These are some of the most important benefits of second-generation CRM applications in the cloud:

- Access to the latest releases, services, and innovations in CRM
- Access to online resources of customer information that enables the company to gain a better insight into the situation and market trends, integration with public and private online forums, and new tools to increase productivity and better web communication are just a few examples of cloud computing technology that the company can use to improve customer relationships
- Flexible ways of accessing CRM applications means that users can access the same applications simultaneously and perform the necessary updates remotely
- Ease of use for both key and *ordinary* CRM applications, because cloud services can be used by everyone through their usual internet browser, and cloud resources are available in the same way
- Better utilization of employees' potential, because employees are free from system maintenance and various other tasks, so they can focus on other more complex tasks
- Improved relationship between price and value of CRM system, because there is no need to buy hardware and software, so that money can be spent on other things.

Business continuity

When it comes to ensuring business continuity and recovery after a severe break from work, many small and medium-sized organizations in the past have been unable to afford to design, build, and maintain their own business continuity system. Thanks to cloud computing, today's business can achieve better continuity and safer recovery after they encounter violent termination of work. In the event of a violent interruption of work due to a natural disaster, the service provider restores the server client companies as virtual providers in their environment. These services enable system recovery within minutes or hours, with minimal loss of data, all at no cost except for the regular subscription to the cloud.

The benefits of using such business continuity and recovery services after violent termination are as follows:

- Service prices are completely transparent and based on subscription.
- The subscription covers all software, infrastructure, and services needed to deliver solutions.

- Activation is quick and easy—most of the configuration to be restored can be done via the internet.
- This minimizes the risk of overflowing.
- In the case of traditional services, such service providers give more clients the same IT resources and avoid subscribing clients from the same region to the same equipment, but it may be that several clients who are searching for system restore services that cannot be provided to everyone will appear at the same time. Such a situation cannot be completely avoided even in the use of cloud computing, but the risk here is nevertheless minimal, because many more clients can share the same physical space.
- Reduced costs of testing a recovery plan after a violent interruption.

A recovery plan after a violent interruption should be tested in practice. Traditional service providers have typically made such tests expensive, because they have heavily burdened their resources. Providers of such cloud computing services are much more rational towards clients, allowing them to periodically test recovery plans either for free or for a minimum fee.

Exploring the possible Oracle CX deployments

Every solution before it is used needs to be deployed in the best manner to support the business and workloads. Oracle CX can be deployed in the following two deployment types:

- Cloud deployment
- Hybrid deployment

Cloud deployment is an easier case, since Oracle CX is cloud-based offering. Hybrid deployment, even though it is more complicated, is more prevalent in corporate environments.

Prerequisite knowledge of deployment

For us to be able to consider different deployment types, first, we need to discuss and explain subjects and underlying technologies.

Demilitarized zone

A **demilitarized zone** (**DMZ**) denotes a specific area of territory between two opposing forces. It prohibits any form of military activity—whether it is a special operation, sabotage, or spying.

Today, it is unlikely you will find any company or organization without a computer. And where there are computers, there is an internal local network that unites them. By itself, the presence of a common internal local network is very practical and safe. But with the appearance of the **World Wide Web** (**WWW**), it became a bit more complicated. Now the vast majority of companies use WWW services. This greatly facilitates workflow, because everyone can find all the information they need within a matter of seconds.

However, with the development of the internet, there was a threat of penetration into the company's general local network. These concerned companies have public internet services which are available to every user of the web. The danger was that the attacker, after accessing the web service, could also access personal data stored on any computer connected to the internal network. This has caused a series of difficulties to be solved by the creation of a DMZ.

From the initial interpretation of the term, it becomes clear to us that the DMZ is a special area, which prohibits any kind of harmful activity. We need to be aware that the DMZ's idea is a very simple solution that creates a separate segment of the computer network, isolated from all external internet hosts and from the company's internal network. It is also a control restriction or a complete ban on internet access and the internal network.

Creating a separate segment of the network is easy. For this purpose, firewalls are used. The word **firewall** for an average user can bring to mind movies about famous hackers, but few people know what it actually does.

A firewall is a hardware and software unit of a computer network that allows filtering of incoming network traffic by default of the operator (administrator) rules. Also, in the case of unauthorized intrusion, the attacker accesses only files that are within the secret sector, without prejudice to others.

There are at least two types of DMZ configurations.

In the first configuration, the firewall divides the network into three sectors:

- The internal network
- The DMZ
- The internet channel

However, this method doesn't ensure sufficient protection. Most large companies still use another method—with a large number of firewalls. In that case, the attacker will have to overcome at least one additional perimeter of the system with its own traffic filter, which greatly increases security.

Firewall

A firewall can also prevent your computer from sending malware to other computers. Firewalls are usually the first and fundamental method of increasing the security of the computer system. The firewall examines whether the packet traffic between a computer or a network meets certain criteria. If it does, the packets are missed, and if not, traffic stops. The firewall can re-examine the packets by different criteria—for example, by their starting and destination addresses or the number of ports they use, by specific types of traffic, that is, the protocols used, by the attributes or status of the packet, and so on.

Many companies that have an internal computer network are using some of the firewall solutions, most often combined with hardware and software solutions.

Firewalls are divided into two types (the main difference between these two types is in their use and not in the technology they use):

- **Business**: A circuit or software solution (or combination) that protects the entire business network from potentially harmful traffic in such a way that all network traffic is redirected through a dedicated device intended only for that purpose
- **Private**: Usually, a software solution that protects the user's computer on which it is located

The firewall is responsible for several important things within the information system:

- It must implement a security policy
- If a particular property is not allowed, it must disable the work in that sense
- Suspicious events should be recorded
- It should warn the administrator of attempts to break through and compromise the security policy
- In some cases, it may allow usage statistics

One of the major disadvantages of a firewall is the slowing down of network traffic due to filtering.

Connectors

Data integration in the cloud enables the simple communication, exchange, and improvement of various data processes. Communication between various sources and data points takes place using easily accessible cloud architecture for embedded connectors.

Transformations of input data and their processing uses cloud storage and metadata patterns. The processing uses remote access to the available resources within the cloud, and the speed of the process depends primarily on the quality of the connection used. The additional impact of the lack of storage space, the amount of free disk space, and the burden on the existing local cloud infrastructure has been completely eliminated. Sources and data destinations process structured and unstructured data at the same speed, providing simple possibilities for extracting the necessary information from the input components regardless of the shape and structure of data obtained at the source.

Regardless of the model applied, simplicity and speed of access and reduced maintenance costs are just some of the key features that confirm the benefits of data integration in the cloud and its growing popularity.

In today's internet era, the data is found all around us, and users create, modify, exchange, and refresh using applications and systems typically located in the cloud.

In this way, the cloud becomes a centralized platform for the exchange of information between heterogeneous systems and applications using remote access. That is why the importance of data integration in the cloud is even greater. Since all systems, programs, and related infrastructure are located in the cloud, there are no more installation, maintenance, and licensing costs, nor additional costs of adding new users. With an ease of access and scalability, memory and storage problems are solved by placing data on remote servers. In this way, local infrastructure reduces the load created by the lack of storage space, and with the appropriate conditions, you can gain insight into the performance of the allocated cloud space (server and related architecture).

In the event of a need to increase storage space, the currently-used cloud infrastructure is simply expanded by the addition of new resources. Data storage is provided with low maintenance costs, and data backup is achieved in a simple way with low maintenance costs, as data is stored within a centralized data center with the appropriate back up and process options (depending on the business requirements of the company).

All data patterns, sources, and destinations are configured in a simple way using a large number of connectors that, regardless of the choice of integration, will enable a fully integrated environment for full functionality.

Oracle Integration Cloud Services

Oracle **Integration Cloud Services** (**ICS**) is used for the more complex integration of applications, in our case, Oracle CX solutions.

The main features of this include the following:

- **Pre-defined integration flows**: Instead of re-defining the integration flows that are most commonly used, such as those between trade applications (CRMs) and the configuration, pricing, and CPC applications, Oracle offers you predefined integration flows between applications that include Oracle CX.

- **Oracle mechanical learning-based learning recommendations**: This will speed up the whole process of designing and delivering integration, because you can get referrals for integration, mapping data, and other issues in real time and thus reduce the number of errors.

- **Automatic self-repair**: Recognizes and applies updates to make your integration and processes available and functioning without interruption.

- **Process automation**: Automate comprehensive business processes with a simple platform that simplifies the everyday tasks your users and employees perform within the workflow. You can model all models, from simple workflows to advanced structures or case management, in one tool.

- **Self-initiative**: Provides recommendations based on machine learning and the **next best action** to prevent errors associated with complex mapping of data between applications and to get the best user selections for the process flows. Process templates shorten integration to make business services available faster and at lower prices.

- **Connect your digital employees**: Optimize your daily digital workforce activities through a multi-channel experience that coordinates tasks of different people, systems, and robots (robotic process automation).

- **Easily develop applications for mobile devices and the web**: Quickly build and manage mobile and web applications with a declarative development environment that is managed visually, by dragging and dropping, and automatically generated by the application code. You will have full access to the code so you can upgrade and modify it.

- **Direct posting**: When ready, you can share your application with the rest of the world (or just to a specific group of users) with one mouse click. Visual Builder serves your application through a self-administering hosted platform.

- **Self-managed**: Visual Builder manages the development and deployment platforms for your developers and users. You only need a browser—the platform automatically manages the implementation and execution of the code in the background and foreground.

Deploying the Cloud

In this deployment type, **Sales Cloud** has a central role in CX solution. All of the company's customer and contact information is stored in **Sales Cloud** and **Sales Cloud** orchestrates all other parts of the CX solution.

As outlined in the following diagram, the whole CRM/CX workload is processed by Oracle CX solutions. The central point is allocated to the Oracle Sales Cloud that handles data flow between on premises systems and orchestrates data flow between Oracle CX solutions:

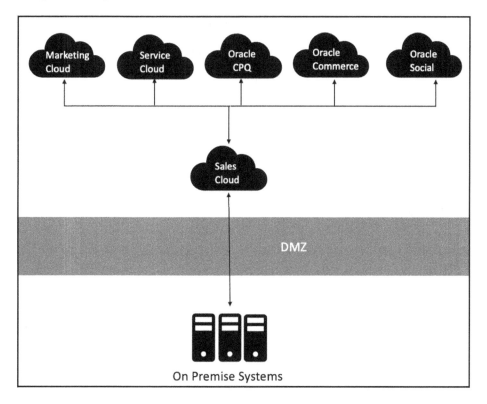

Since the whole solution is based in the cloud, it means that all of the customer data and associated workflows are outside your organization and in the cloud. Because of this fact, it is important that the organization selects an appropriate region so that no legal issues arise.

Communication between CX cloud and on premises is minimal, and all data is stored and secured in the cloud. This means that even in the event of a catastrophic accident in the company's hosting center, the CX solution will continue functioning unaffected.

This, too, has some advantages and challenges. Let us understand both here.

Some benefits of cloud deployment are listed as follows:

- There is no CX infrastructure to maintain
- There is high availability and disaster recovery
- Data backups are created
- Implementation is quick
- Scalability

Some disadvantages of cloud deployment are as follows:

- Harder migration path when compared to hybrid deployment
- Potential legal and security issues
- Account administration is usually more complex
- Less flexible solution than hybrid cloud deployment
- Less control

Simple hybrid deployment

A hybrid deployment entails that a part of the solution workflows is going through the company's systems. In this case, the company already has an on premises CRM system (for example, Siebel) and the company would like to utilize it as a part of a CX solution.

As outlined in the following diagram, the on premises CRM is the processing part of the workload, which is supplemented by Oracle CX cloud solutions. The on premises CRM is orchestrating the data flow between on premises systems and Oracle CX solutions. In this deployment type, we use Oracle CX as an extension of an **On Premises CRM**, providing functionalities that are lacking or are not fit for the business purposes:

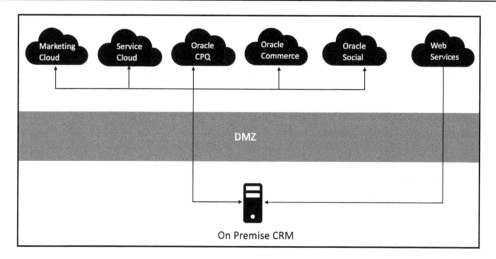

As shown in our architecture, Sales Cloud is not a part of it anymore; instead, on premises CRM is coordinating and utilizing functionalities of Oracle CX solutions.

Because of the complexity of this solution, in case of the catastrophic accident in the company's hosting center, the CX solution will not continue functioning unaffected.

Since customer and contact data is stored in on premises CRM systems, the probability of data loss is higher than in other deployment types.

Some of the benefits of complex hybrid deployment are as follows:

- An easier migration path when compared to pure cloud deployment
- Because not all data is stored in the cloud, this means fewer potential legal and security issues
- Account administration is easier
- A more flexible solution than pure cloud deployment
- A higher amount of control when compared to cloud deployment

Some disadvantages of simple hybrid deployment are listed as follows:

- Parts of the infrastructure still require administration
- Not all information is automatically backed-up
- Slower implementation
- Less scalable when compared to pure cloud deployment
- Complex networking and integrations are required for a solution to function
- Possible firewall issues

Complex hybrid deployment

Expanding further on the previous deployment type, we have introduced Oracle ICS as a part of our solution. Oracle ICS has out-of-the-box connectors that simplify integration and orchestration of workflows between on premises and Oracle CX solutions.

As outlined in our diagram, on premises systems are processing part of the workload, which is supplemented by Oracle CX cloud solutions.

Since this kind of deployment usually entails complex integrations and data flows, we have added Oracle ICS to our solutions. Oracle ICS integrates on premises solutions with Oracle CX cloud and orchestrates data flow between Oracle CX solutions:

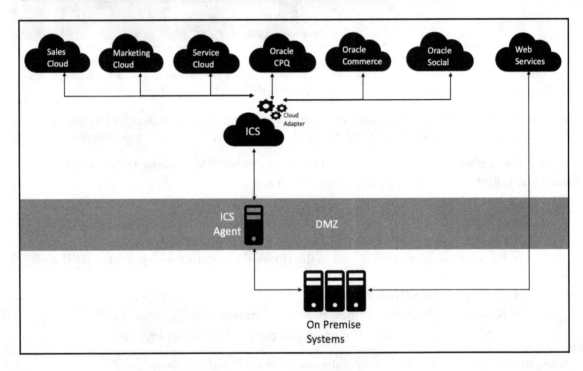

This is the most complex hybrid deployment case that we will discuss.

In this case, on premises systems are handling the part of workflows and communication with web services located outside the company. Because of the complexity of processes and complex integrations, we have introduced ICS alongside **ICS Agent**. **ICS Agent** is a server application that must be located in the **DMZ** of the company, and it is used to manage a connection between ICS and the company's backend systems.

Workflows originate from various systems and are accordingly distributed to the appropriate Oracle CX solution.

Because of the complexity of this solution, in a case of a catastrophic accident in the company's hosting center, a CX solution will not continue functioning unaffected.

Since customer and contact data is stored in Sales Cloud, the probability of data loss is low, depending on what data is available only in on premises systems.

Let's list some of the benefits of complex hybrid deployment, as follows:

- An easier migration path when compared to pure cloud deployment
- Because not all data is stored in the cloud, this means fewer potential legal and security issues
- Account administration is easier
- More flexible solution than pure cloud deployment
- Highest possible amount of control

The disadvantages of complex hybrid deployment are listed as follows:

- Parts of the infrastructure still require administration
- Not all information is automatically backed up
- Slower implementation
- Less scalable when compared to pure cloud deployment
- Most complex networking and integrations are required for the solution to function
- Possible numerous firewall issues

In the next section, we will discuss how to choose the best possible deployment model for your CX deployment and what are important variables to consider.

Choosing an appropriate deployment model

Oracle CX is an extremely flexible package of solutions that can be tailored to support any type of business and size of the company. The size of the company, needs, and resources should be the main variables to consider when choosing deployment type:

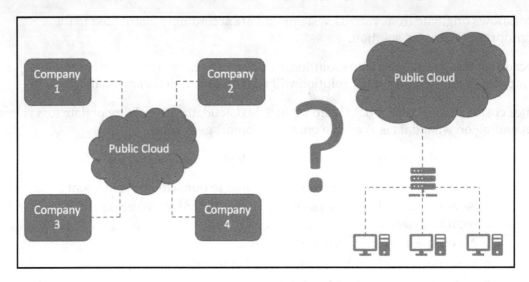

In general terms, smaller companies are better off with pure cloud deployment, while larger or corporate companies are better off with hybrid deployment.

The main advantage of pure cloud deployment is that the company does not require any up-front investment but is sacrificing some flexibility.

In the case of larger companies or corporations, the company has already made an investment in systems, and, usually, processes and workflows are more complex. Therefore, hybrid deployment is usually a better solution, since it provides much more flexibility and easier migration and adoption in an organization.

Complexities that arise with hybrid development are better managed with a larger organization that has more resources at its disposal and more guidelines and procedures to protect it from legal and security problems.

Summary

Cloud computing has been accepted around the world and is increasingly being used for business and private purposes. Today, organizations are increasingly using the internet to do their jobs. The cloud allows them to avoid buying the necessary hardware and software, and with a very reasonable price, we rent all hardware and software and do their job, which enables them to reduce costs and flexibility in their work, and a faster performance.

As almost every household uses the internet today, it is so important for organizations to have their business or part of the business on the internet in order to be as popular and spacious as possible and to do the best they can. But cloud computing has not yet reached its climax, continues to evolve, and is trying to reduce security issues and increase the economic aspect in order to attract as many users as possible.

In the future, we can expect that cloud computing will encourage the development of more advanced technologies and how they will improve both business and general use of computing for private purposes.

In this chapter, the aim was to get acquainted with the application of cloud computing for business purposes and all its characteristics, advantages and disadvantages.

The result is that cloud computing leads to easier and quicker operation compared to traditional business, with a reduction in costs, which means fewer employees in the organization and no hardware and software, because it is all hired by the service providers. But this kind of computing has downsides, including issues with privacy and data security, data management, data availability, and so on.

In the next chapter, we will utilize all the knowledge discussed in previous chapters and design a CX solution for the TELCO company.

Section 4: Use Case
4

This section will explain one use case for how you can utilize the whole Oracle CX suite.

The following chapter will be covered in this section:

- Chapter 8, *Case Study – Oracle CX Cloud*

Case Study - Oracle CX Cloud

8

Customer experience (**CX**) is not an IT concept, though many in IT are encountering it because of its intensive use of new IT technologies. CX is defined as a system that adjusts strategy, organization, and business culture in such a way that all contact with the user leads to the long-term satisfaction of the user, and thus the long-term profit of the company.

In developed economies, in the vigorous market battle for each user, CX quickly proved to be an important factor in attracting users, and companies that succeeded in adopting it gained a market advantage that enabled them to quickly recover their CX investment. CX needs to be integrated into the entire process of customer experience, from initial contact to end-to-end purchasing, and marketing, sales, and customer support must be integrated through IT.

CX should not to be considered as *what we can offer to a user,* but rather *how to identify their needs.* Oracle CX has solutions that address specific areas of the customer journey and together they provide best possible customer experience. This is depicted here:

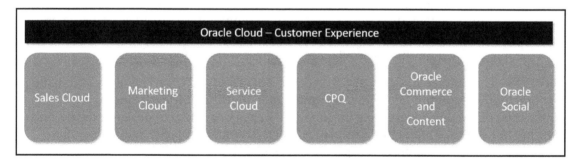

Moving towards a customer-centric way of thinking is crucial. While posing the first question, *what can we offer to a user*, we remain focused on ourselves and the services we offer, trying to find a market for these services. Instead, we need to start thinking in a different way. We should identify the needs of each individual user and adjust the services we offer according to their needs.

Telecommunication companies (TELCOs) usually represent the most challenging case for CX implementations, since users can easily change operators and the market is saturated with service providers.

All offers on a market are usually very similar and there is no more case of locking phone brands to a specific provider. In sum, all of this means that the only tool left for a TELCO to use is **customer experience**, by striving to deliver the best possible customer journey as a differentiating factor.

Since the number of users is very large for the implementation of CX in a TELCO, it is necessary to use modern IT technologies and techniques that allow the personalization of user relations regardless of the total number of users. This means that fundamental changes must be made in the structure of the TELCO so that it can adopt CX, which, of course, represents a significant investment.

CX Implementation

CX is not a one-time commitment, but a process that is constantly being repeated and improved. Each cycle begins with the acquisition of the relevant critical knowledge about the users, that is, a detailed analysis of their behavior, habits, wishes, and needs. To put it simply, users are segmented on the basis of certain common features, identifying the most profitable users, the users who have the potential to become profitable to the relationship with them is invested in, and those who are no longer worth investing in.

The first level of implementation of CX is called **operational CX**, and involves automating and optimizing the entire sales process (contracting, meetings, bidding, and so on), automating marketing by applying information systems designed to design, execute, and measure the effects of marketing campaigns, track customer contacts, and, ultimately, automating customer support through the call center.

Continuous innovation and a unique value for users is also an integral part of CX.

Services must be changed and enriched in accordance with the needs of users, and companies must have the ability to recognize their needs before they are clearly expressed.

User segmentation is the most technologically demanding part of CX. It involves integrating all relevant customer data, from both transaction systems and external data sources, into a single data warehouse, and then exploiting the data stored with various OLAP tools, statistical packets, using the data digging method, and so on. This is also the most critical part of the entire CX cycle, as the users that are selected will be analyzed for their needs, and it represents the second phase of the CX implementation, called **analytical CX**. Knowledge gained in this way is then exploited when designing marketing campaigns for the selected users. Which approach is best for them? Which services and channels do users consume?

The last step in the implementation cycle is effective interaction with customers—not only marketing campaigns but also responding to user feedback at the same time, gathering information about how users react to a particular action.

To summarize, CX is a cycle that consists of three repeated steps:

1. Gaining customer knowledge
2. Taking actions based on that knowledge
3. Collecting the results of the action and combining them with the pre-existing knowledge to create new knowledge

With this approach, telecommunications companies can benefit from a competitive advantage, simplified internal organization by shortening the duration of information exchange cycles, and eliminating unproductive information flows, and increased profits.

TELCO case description

In today's world, technological development and innovation is progressing at an astonishing rate. The life cycle of a product or a service is not measured in years anymore, but in weeks or months. Each month, a multitude of devices are released in the market, and they are fashion/status statements to the same degree as communication devices. Data usage is exploding exponentially. The amount of information exchanged each second is exploding, driven by cloud-based IT models and mobile device usage.

This change in the technological landscape is also driving a change in customer behavior. Many long-standing behaviors have been changed forever, such as the way we communicate, the way we access resources, how we share information, and how we influence our society. These changes have also changed customer expectations regarding purchasing and service consumption. Customers need to use multiple channels to complete transactions, such as web, mobile, email, social networks, and in store.

This shift has resulted in customers' influence surpassing the company's influence; in other words, customers today value more what they read in social media than what the company communicates in commercials. Today's customer expects that experiences across all channels are seamless and companies cannot afford to use a channel-specific approach, since this approach is fragmented and can lead to poor customer experience.

In sum, the challenges faced by a TELCO today can be split into the following three main groups:

- Technological
- Behavioral
- Expectation management

The need to focus on customer experience and customer journey is not being pushed forward by companies, but by customer expectations and demand. Customers demand more options and choices from companies. Services need to be easily accessible over multiple channels. Customers also want to be able to easily express their opinions and views, especially critical ones, and they are expecting companies to acknowledge them. This creates pressure to tailor positive communication with customers.

Creating customer experience

According to numerous studies, customers will pay more for a better customer experience, which represents a real hurdle for TELCOs since they are always perceived as the companies with the lowest customer satisfaction rating.

Business objectives for TELCOs can be grouped into three categories:

- Expanding customer base
- Reducing churn
- Increasing operational efficiency

TELCOs need to be able to acquire the largest possible number of customers, with the lowest possible cost of acquisition. Everybody knows that retention is cheaper than acquisition, and that is why customer retention and building relationships with existing customers is a primary concern. Added challenges are keeping the costs down and getting an adequate level of profitability.

The best way of achieving those goal is to increase operational efficiency and transition to automated communication and channels:

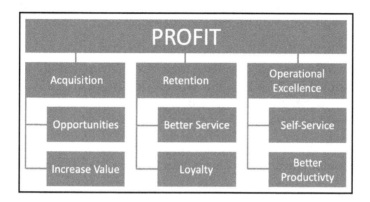

In the preceding diagram, we can see the main areas that influence the profit acquired by a company. It outlines the fact that companies need to focus externally on customers and internally on operational excellence, which is actually a supporting activity for acquisition and retention.

Acknowledging that influence has shifted from companies to customers, appropriate CX is critical for a company to be able to achieve these goals. But how can a TELCO address customer needs in a market that is becoming more and more competitive and with increasing customer expectations?

To address customer needs and to be ahead of the competition, the company must adopt a holistic approach.

The holistic approach and its challenges

The customer, by the nature of things, does not need to have specific knowledge in the field in which the company does its business. However, even if there is no previous experience with the organization and its products, a successful holistic marketing approach allows the customer, from the very first moment when entering the point of sale of the requested business entity, to look at TV commercials and/or search for the corporate Facebook page and recognize the professional aspects and value criteria of the company.

It is, therefore, extremely important that an organization consisting of a number of more or less autonomous business units—such as marketing and sales, corporate and general affairs, human resources, finance, and the sector of strategy and development, for example—comes to a qualitatively higher level of mutual communication and coordination of activities.

Thus, for example, marketing and sales have to co-operate very closely with the development department in order to define and create a product that would be attractive to current and potential customers. Human resources, on the other hand, have to be consulted to engage adequate and well-trained marketing associates.

Finance and accounting should be in regular communication with the marketing and sales sector in order to provide the necessary resources to cover the advertising activities of the enterprise.

From all this, it follows that the keyword in the holistic approach to marketing is *communication*. This implies a harmonized information system within the organization. Strengthening internal marketing communications enables not only a timely flow of information but also motivates employees to perform their tasks, regardless of their heterogeneity, as consumer-oriented experts.

To be able to adopt a holistic approach, the company needs to be able to recognize two key aspects:

- Customer experience is a journey
- Customer experience impacts the entire business

Once the company understands these two aspects, they will be able to deliver the best possible customer experience and achieve their business goals.

The TELCO's CX implementation

Customer experience consists of people, technology, and underlying processes. All of these building blocks need to be connected directly to the customer experience. It is also important that managers at all levels understand how their own work is connected to the company's customer experience efforts. This understanding enables all levels of the company to perform their tasks in the best possible way to support customer experience efforts.

CX implementation projects are usually hindered by resistance to changes from within the organization. It is essential that the implementation plan addresses this aspect with utmost diligence. Managing the strategy implementation process implies a good combination of the various factors and elements that contribute to the achievement of strategic goals.

The implementation process can be facilitated by certain factors. The question is how to diagnose and find those factors that will have a decisive impact on the quality of the process. The issue is even more complex if you analyze the scope and variety of problems that arise in the process. Therefore, it is necessary to focus on those elements that actively participate in the implementation and to try to see what is needed for them to do so.

Prerequisites for successful implementation

The purpose of IT solutions is to support business processes and procedures and to understand them in order to create a baseline for your implementation. It is important to understand which existing IT solutions and their corresponding processes will be removed, and which ones cannot be removed and therefore need to be integrated and adjusted to support new solutions.

Before starting the implementation of your new architecture, there are some prerequisites that need to be considered:

- Assessing processes and procedures
- Assessing IT infrastructure
- Assessing what of your existing software will be retained
- Assessing users and roles
- Preparing data
- Setting up reporting

The usual reason for implementing new solutions is to support new processes and procedures, which means that new user groups with appropriate roles and privileges need to be created. In this phase of planning, security must be at the top of the list, and the least privilege principle should be asserted.

For a new solution to operate optimally, data must be prepared. Data that has no value should be removed and data quality and accuracy must be assured.

Analysis

To be able to conduct appropriate analysis, it is imperative to structure the gap analysis in an appropriate way while having sufficient time and resources. The best practice in gap analysis is to hire external resources, because that will provide an impartial view of the company and facilitate interdepartmental cooperation.

The analysis should clarify the following:

- The company's stance regarding CX
- What is currently being done right and what is missing or being ignored
- The impact of these deficiencies on business
- Gaps from both customers and employees perspective
- Overall qualitative and quantitative impacts

Let's assume that the gaps that were identified during this process are as follows:

Nr.	Gap Description	GAP Severity Minor/Normal/Major	GAP Priority 1-5 (1Highest, 5 Lowest)
1.	Current interaction points are not easy for customers to use. Customers invest more time in understanding applications than using them.	Major	1
2.	Functionalities are unique to channel, there is no unified customer experience.	Major	1
3.	Current thinking and initiatives in company are compartmentalized and only address issues of some parts of the business.	Major	1
4.	Current systems are not integrated, resulting in fragmented customer experience.	Major	1
5.	Time to Market of current campaigns is below industry standard.	Major	1
6.	Look and feel of applications is not unified with brand representation in retail.	Normal	3

This is only a small representation of the results of the analysis. We will address major gaps with a gap priority of **1**.

Strategy

The strategy must be translated into concrete action, and this action must be carefully implemented.

The strategy is implemented in three mutually dependent phases:

- Identification of measurable commonly set annual goals
- Development of special functional strategies
- Development and binding of concise policies for decision-making

In addition to the organizational structure and processes for the successful implementation of the company's strategy, there is also a significant correlation between strategy and organizational culture.

Organizational culture represents a set of basic assumptions with which the group, through a learning process, addresses the interference of external adaptation and internal integration of the enterprise, and then presents them with the new member as the right way to discover and solve problems.

More simply, organizational culture is defined as an integral system of norms, values, performance, assumptions, and symbols that determine the behavior of, and response to, the problems of all employees and thus shapes the appearance of an enterprise.

In addition to the previously mentioned coverage, organizational culture is also of great importance for new associates in the company.

Everyone who joins the company's knowledge of organizational culture is a tool for easier engagement in business. Analyzing and shaping the organizational culture requires a systematic approach. In most cases, such an approach consists of the following:

- Analysis of existing organizational culture
- Evaluation stages where we find discrepancies between the existing organizational culture and the company's strategy
- Phases of design through which we change or support existing organizational culture

All of the goals and requirements must align with the overall company strategy.

Requirements

We will define requirements in a similar way that we have described in previous chapters. In this requirement, we have outlined the rationale behind the need for a unified customer experience:

	Requirement 1: Unified customer experience
Statement	Functionalities and responsibilities across all channels must be defined
Rationale	The company must provide consistent and seamless interaction across all contact points with the customer
Implications	The customer will have the same experience regardless of the type of contact point

Here, we have explained requirements that are connected to unified customer experience, and added a requirement that applications need to be easy to use:

	Requirement 2: Easy to use
Statement	The solution is easy to use for customers and employees
Rationale	The more time that is needed to invest in understanding applications, and the more time that users need to invest in understanding how to use applications, the less incentive they have to use them
Implications	The solution must adopt a common look and feel that encompasses all of the components of the solution

In this requirement, we are outlining that the whole company must work as one so that the best possible customer experience is provided to customers:

	Requirement 3: Integrations
Statement	All of the systems incorporated in a CX solution must be integrated so that they are able to provide a unified experience for customers and a unified view about them
Rationale	Integrations need to adhere to SOA principles so that they are able to support the changes to support agile businesses needs in an appropriate manner
Implications	A shift from system-centric to a customer-centric mode

In this requirement, we have explained that all functionalities must be available and the same across all channels:

	Requirement 4: Omni-channel support
Statement	Functionalities should not be unique to a specific channel, but they should be general in their nature.
Rationale	TTM is much lower if functionalities are general in their nature. Functionalities are the same across all the channels.
Implications	Common monitoring and management solutions need to be implemented for each of the channels. The functionalities defined need to be feasible across all the channels.

In this requirement, we are explaining that anything that needs to be done in organization must be done in a secure manner:

	Requirement 5: Security first
Statement	A comprehensive and centrally administered security solution is needed
Rationale	A lack of centralized security without a unified view and reporting, increases the risk of security incidents
Implications	The company will need to implement centralized security and IAM solution

This requirement addresses the actual benefits of unified experience and ease of use, that is, they need to secure the maximum benefit for the organization:

	Requirement 6: Maximize benefits
Statement	Decisions are made to provide maximum benefit to the enterprise
Rationale	Decisions made for the benefit of the whole enterprise have higher value than decisions made for the benefit of a single part of the organization
Implications	Priorities for solution definition and adoption must be established for the whole enterprise

In this section, we have outlined the main requirements that will be the cornerstone of our architecture and implementation plan.

Architecture

The implementation architecture consists of two levels, logical and solution architecture. Firstly, we will describe solutions used in Oracle CX, then explain the logical solution, and finally, we will present solution architecture.

Products used

Some of the products that are used in the solution architecture are as follows:

- **Oracle Social Cloud**: This enables your company to collaborate effectively both internally and externally and become a social company, in which every part of your company influences your objectives. Oracle Social Cloud is integrated out of the box with Oracle Sales Cloud, Oracle Marketing Cloud, Oracle Service Cloud, and Oracle Commerce Cloud, enabling you to constantly innovate and find new ways to forward your business objectives.

- **Oracle Commerce Cloud**: This is an extensive and unified solution for companies which engage in B2B and B2C operations. It has myriad advanced features and, when paired with other solutions in Oracle CX, offers benefits and contributes to the overall architecture. It represents your storefront.

- **Oracle CPQ Cloud**: This is a process within the sales life cycle. Each business that sells complicated products incorporates a **configure, price, and quote** (**CPQ**) method in one way or another. Once a client is curious about a product, the salesperson should put together a quote to satisfy the customer's request.

- **Oracle Service Cloud**: This provides companies with a unified interface that enables them to monitor and engage with customers over any channel that is available to you. Since it is a part of the Oracle CX suite, it enables you to easily integrate with other offerings and unlock the full potential of your CX environment.

- **Oracle Responsys**: This is used to manage and orchestrate marketing interactions with their customers across email, mobile, social, display, and the web.

- **Oracle Eloqua**: This is used for marketing automation, that is, for creating personalized campaigns across multiple channels. Oracle Eloqua comes with support for 500 partners, comprising 700 integrations, which can be used in your campaigns.

- **Oracle BlueKai**: This is used for marketing data management. It enables you to understand the data that you have gathered in your campaigns. Essentially, it is a cloud-based big data platform.

- **Oracle Infinity**: This is used for marketing data analytics. It is an analytics platform used for tracking, measuring, and optimizing visitor behavior on your sites and apps.

- **Oracle Sales Cloud**: This is an Oracle offering with the closest resemblance to CX in the Oracle CX suite. It can be used as a standalone solution and can do all tasks reasonably well, but the real power of Oracle CX suite is unlocked if it is paired with other solutions.
- **Oracle Commerce**: This can be used to design your pages and web stores, easily maintain them, and change them in an agile manner to respond to market needs. The same site is optimized for mobile devices and computer screens. Another significant feature of this solution is B2B capabilities, which enables your company's business to business collaboration.
- **Oracle Right Now Web Experience**: This is a self-service platform that enables your customers to manage their options, subscriptions, contact data, submit cases, and more. What they can manage depends on your design. The perfect case would be to allow customers to change their subscription. Subscriptions should be stored in Oracle Sales Cloud and when the customers log in, it should be acquired using an API call and presented to the customer alongside all the subscriptions the customer can migrate to. The last step should be the customer's verification of changes, and data changes in Oracle Sales Cloud through API calls.
- **Oracle Right Now Contact Centre Experience**: This functionality enables you to manage communication with customers through a unified interface. If paired with Oracle Field Service, it can help you to facilitate communication between your technician teams and customers.

Logical view

We can identify four logical layers that will enable us to create engaging interaction with customers, rather than a purely transactional one. The four layers of CX experience are as follows:

- **Interaction layer**—consists of front-office applications, including both assisted and unassisted channels.
- **Coordination layer**—consists of front-office applications that enable seamless cross-channel support, sales, knowledge management, and customer data.
- **Order management layer**—consists of customer-facing back-office applications that enable order management, order delivery, personalized interaction, offers, and products.

- **Order fulfilment layer**—consists of back-office applications with which customers usually do not have any contact. Applications in this layer usually support fulfillment, workforce management, and supply chain management:

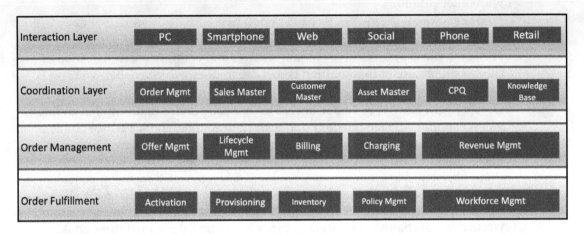

This logical view of the architecture addresses the four main points that are critical for great customer experience.

Solution architecture

The solution architecture should be flexible and modular so that processes can be adjusted as quickly as possible when there is a business need, that is, a lower **time to market** (**TTM**), while being stable and ensuring business continuity.

Two main goals that the solution should provide are as follows:

- Cross-channel support with unified customer experience
- Timely order management and fulfillment processes

Cross-channel support architecture

Cross-channel support solution establishes channel coordination, knowledge management, sales catalog, **Self-Service**, **Retail**, and automatic decision-making functionalities:

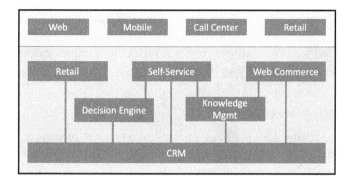

This architecture outlines a solution that provides cross-channel experience and support. It shows all of the important parts/systems that need to work as one, so that consistent customer experience is available on each device.

Order management and fulfillment management architecture

Order management and fulfillment management play an integral part in providing exceptional customer experience. They ensure fast service activation, provision, and order management. These processes are the Achilles' heel of many modern businesses:

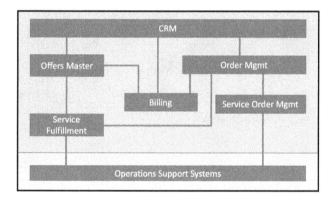

This architecture is an especially good fit for Oracle OSS, but because it is general, it can work with any other OSS solution. It outlines all of the supporting systems that need to be in place and integrated so that business processes that the customer does not see, but are essential, are operating in the best possible manner.

Unified solution architecture

The unified solution architecture is developed using a holistic approach, and this enables the company to engage with customers across various points and also addresses the operational aspect of the business processes.

This solution architecture addresses both front-office and back-office aspects:

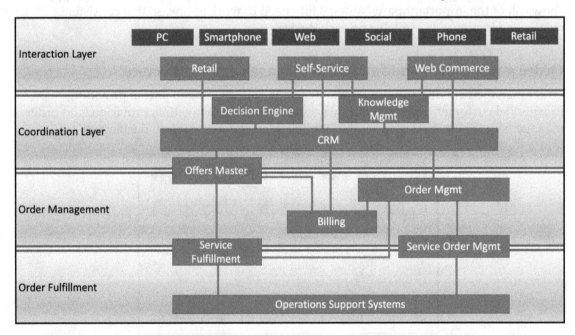

This architecture provides a comprehensive set of functionalities related to CX, but at the same time, it is flexible enough to accommodate any change that business will encounter in the future.

These are the main points of the architecture:

- Cross-channel support—This will enable the company to offer unified customer experience across all possible interaction points with customers
- Personalized offers—These will enable the company to nurture its relationship with customers and make them feel appreciated by offering them relevant products and services
- Faster TTM—This will enable the company to enter the market faster with new promotions, products, and services

This architecture improves customer experience across all of the interaction points and facilitates all of the business processes.

Mapping of the products used

When considering marketing and loyalty, the primary factor to take into account is product marketing. A goal of product marketing is to design and implement a consistent and all-encompassing experience across all devices. In our use case, these components are a part of the **Need** and **Recommend** phases.

The main goal of marketing is to create a need for services, and/or products, with the goal of establishing customer loyalty. The best indicator of customer loyalty to a company is through word-of-mouth regarding the company's services and products. The best outcome of loyalty is the generation of word-of-mouth about a company's services/products.

Communication via social media needs to be two-way interaction. Social media enables companies to build engagement and promote companies services/products.

The main purpose of this solution architecture is to provide self-service functionalities, including all information regarding orders to customers.

Another objective is also to provide support to a customer that's accessible through any channel the customer would like to use to contact the company. Examples of this include a knowledge base, chat functionality, integrated communications, ticketing systems, and guided help:

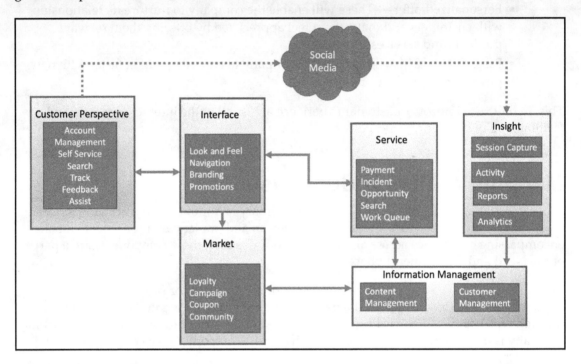

This architecture shows all the areas that are needed to be a part of solution from the customers' perspective and how they communicate together.

The next step is to map these areas to Oracle CX solutions, each encompassing one area:

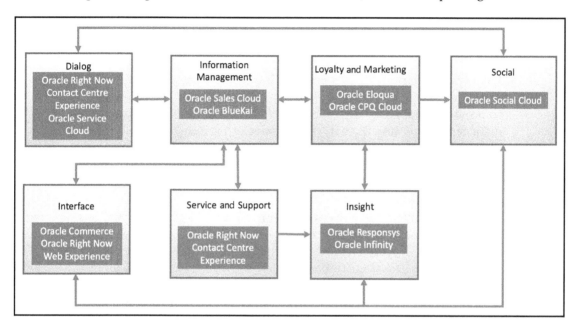

Let's go through what is happening here:

- **Information Management** uses **Oracle Sales Cloud** and **Oracle BlueKai**. Information management will enable the company to create a 360° view of all customers, enrich data, accurately identify customers across devices, share the data with other solutions, and record the data on basis of the device ID. You can also define custom objects in **Oracle Sales Cloud**, while maintaining clean and accurate data.

- The **Interface** uses the storefront functionality of **Oracle Commerce** cloud. The storefront can be easily customized and expanded so that it can suit your business needs. A guided search enables customers to find all relevant information in a simple and easy way. Storefront supports your B2B and B2C business.

- **Loyalty and Marketing** uses **Oracle Eloqua** and **Oracle CPQ Cloud**. This enables your company to automate and personalize marketing activities. To be able to do so provides your company with advanced segmentation and targeting, lead management, sentiment analysis, adaptive campaigns, closed-loop reporting, web analytics, the ability to create offers based on region, complex pricing rules, dynamic promotions based on defined variables, and order executions. In the case of complex sales or discounts, the company can utilize a built-in approval engine.

- **Insight** uses **Oracle Responsys** and **Oracle Infinity**, providing the business with the ability to collect data, draft reports, evaluate and augment data, and analyze data. This can be used to create personalized campaigns, create customer journeys, and increase customer value.

- **Social** provides the company with social tools, facilitating the flow of information between people and companies in real time. A company is able to publish information, conduct marketing campaigns, engage with customers, and tend to brand on social networks. **Social** also provides the company with the option to understand the sentiment and act in a timely manner.

- **Dialog** uses **Oracle Service Cloud**, unifying all your communication channels into one channel in one user interface. Your agents will be able to see all of the cases and communication, supplemented with information from all systems outlined in this solution.

- **Interface** uses **Oracle Right Now Web Experience**, which allows your customers to access self-service tools, access forums, use an interactive guide, get answers from intelligent auto-response, use the knowledge base, and provide feedback. Syndicated knowledge only shows information that is relevant to web-page content. All of these features can be accessed from any device. On the occasion that the customer wants to contact your customer support, they can do so via email, chat, co-browse, or they can phone agents seamlessly from the page.

This solution will enable your company to lower TTM, and use customer feedback and insight functionalities to provide personalized offers while being highly automated and lowering operational costs.

Understanding the critical points of the CX implementation project plan

CX software is not a plug and play IT solution. Its implementation requires a deeper analysis of business processes and project approach. Many companies want to take this opportunity to radically redesign their business processes. Some of the most important factors can be classified into three groups:

- **Technological factors**: Technology development has created new prerequisites for increased adoption of CX systems—integration with other business applications enables the user to access all relevant data from one IT system alone; user interface improvements and access through various devices (smartphone, tablet) bring insight into information in an intuitive way without having to run complex reports; integrated mechanisms for establishing business rules automate manual activities and the like.

- **Project factors**: An assumption that significantly impacts the success of a CX project and the justification of an investment is the alignment of business and IT goals. Apart from a somewhat declarative strategic level, this need is most important at the business process level—business implementation goals need to be mapped to key business processes and identify areas for improvement that IT needs to deliver. Regardless of the price, the technological level or references of a particular software CX solution, if the implementation does not comply with business expectations and process model optimization, IT *for its own sake* will normally not result in a cost-effective investment. Development of project methodologies specializing in the implementation of business IT solutions greatly help to manage CX projects.

- **Business-technological factors**: The development of the concept of cloud computing has enabled a new business model and a reduction in project risks. CX software is one of the pillars of this approach. The development of technology infrastructure on the supplier's side allows access to CX software without the need for classical IT costs (such as licenses, hardware, IT department, and maintenance) with reduced implementation time and rapid prototype development.

Although the final success of the CX project depends on the combination of these categories and the whole range of specifics of the participants in the value chain (user, IT partner, IT solutions manufacturer), the area to which we will pay special attention is the project factors.

Process approach to the implementation

It is impossible to limit customer relationship management activities to certain business processes in advance. CX as a business discipline encompasses almost all key business roles within the company and almost all key business processes. The traditional understanding of CX starts from the marketing, sales, and customer service process.

In terms of a comprehensive business strategy, at the operational level, the concept of CX can be extended to almost all processes that directly or consequently participate in interaction with the user—for example, managing projects in organizations engaged in professional services, business development activities focused on the focus user segment, and the like.

In CX implementation projects, the absence of clear boundaries between *CX processes* and other processes is the biggest challenge in managing the scope of the project. The unintended consequence is the perception of CX solutions as a general good—in which each department sees benefits and how to achieve them, and no one wants to take responsibility for the entire project.

Unclear ownership of the project results in problematic priority management, which leads to compromises and loss of control of the project. The end result is unfulfilled customer expectations and an ineffective project on the developer's side. This situation is just the tip of the project's problems and risks endemic to the big bang implementation of CX—all modules of solutions for all users within the company.

While such an approach can provide benefits to the implementation of packaged out-of-the-box software or in relatively small-scale projects, most projects that involve adjusting to the specifics of user business alternatives are a process or phase approach to implementation.

We can initiate the process approach by building a CX system. It focuses on each segment of the business or a particular group of processes and, ultimately, results in a comprehensive CX solution. Each subsequent phase enables the extension to another group of processes, but also another iteration of the improvements in the system.

Parallel to the development of the system, end users begin to use the first modules and can easily express future requirements. From the side of the project, this approach reduces the risks by allowing the process to remain focused on the clear direction of system development, and within the expected time duration.

Although the total projected time of implementation of all desired functionality will usually be longer than in the case of the *big bang* implementation, the phase approach allows quick realization of the business benefits and business justification of the investment.

Optimization of marketing investments

Automation of marketing activities is one of the constituents of each CX system, but it also provides a good basis for phase implementation. By focusing on marketing activities, the foundation of a future comprehensive CX system is created (segmentation and clearing of the user base, monitoring the history of user interaction, and so on), while the implementation of the project is much shorter than the overall CX project.

Advanced analytics, budgeting, marketing campaign planning, and social networking enable quick performance and recognition of the benefits of implementation.

Alignment of implementation project with a business strategy

The contribution of CX projects to the success of a business strategy concentrate on complete customer satisfaction, as illustrated in the following diagram:

The CX project comprises three phases:

- **Project planning**: Includes goal setting and defining the project team, their activities, and standards related to client value management
- **Effective project development**: The stage in which a manager analyzes the realization and fulfillment of deadlines for different activities
- **Project efficiency evaluation**: Refers to the contribution of the project to the global strategy of the organization

The complexity of a CX project can be determined through the following:

- **Number of companies involved in project**: The complexity of a project increases exponentially with the number of companies involved with the implementation. This problem is even more pronounced in the case of multi-country implementations, in which a company is implementing similar functionalities in each market, because there are many companies involved who have diverging requirements.

  In addition, if the goal is prediction and behavioral planning of clients based on multidimensional analysis information after each interaction with the client, the project must cover a large number of different departments.

- **A Number of CX component components**: This refers to subsystems that will be included in the CX system, such as the transaction processing system, online system communication, storage management, system data, and the like.

The conclusion is that the larger the number of company departments included and the more components are in the CX system, the more realistic the business support strategies, which are geared towards the full satisfaction of the client needs.

CX strategy outline

The customer-oriented company strategy will consist of acquisition of new customers, creation of loyalty programs, and a business model based on profitable customers.

The CX project will contribute to company strategy through a contact center and touch points for customers that increase customer loyalty, and an increased budget for key customers.

The following CX activities will be connected to the project:

- A loyalty program
- Contact center advancements
- Up-selling and cross-selling of products and services

Appropriate customer value management will have the following impact—an increase in customer value by 15%.

The following departments are included in the CX project—Marketing, Sales, IT, HR, and Finance.

Metrics

The three main metrics used in CX are acquisition (increase sales), retention (monetize relationship), and efficiency (leverage investment). These areas should be considered together with the business challenges that are related to each metric. Let us see how these metrics relate to CX:

Increase Sales	Monetize relationship	Leverage Investment
More opportunities	Higher profit	Increase ROI
Brand value	Loyalty	Decrease cost of operations
Market share	Advocacy	Increase Productivity

All of these three metric groups are essential for the company's future. Monetized relationships provide the company with stability; increased sales provides the company with growth opportunities while leveraging investment keeps expenditure in check.

Acquisition (increase sales)

An organization needs to focus on increasing its own customer base by acquiring new customers. This topic can be further developed in three ways:

- More opportunities can be generated with an increased number of visitors and traffic, whether on-site or in physical stores. More visitors means more opportunities for sales. To attract more visitors, the company must develop and maintain a great brand.
- Brand value is usually one of the most important goals of every company. Increasing brand value can also influence customers to interact more with the company.
- Market share is important for every company because it generates stability and growth. Increased market share creates a better market position for the company.

Acquisition KPIs

We will group KPIs into two groups, strategic and operational. KPIs will enable us to measure the progress of acquisition efforts.

Operational KPIs are as follows:

- **Campaign effectiveness**: We will deduct marketing investment from campaign revenue and divide it by marketing investment
- **View of pages per visit**: Average number of page views per unique visitor
- **Shopping cart**: Percentage of customers that have put articles in the shopping cart, but did not complete the purchase
- **Frequency**: Number of page visits by unique customers in a defined amount of time
- **Items per order**: Average number of items in shopping cart per finished order
- **Up-sell and cross-sell**: Percentage of customers that opt in for up-sell or cross-sell offerings
- **Average revenue per user/customer**: Revenue divided by the number of users or customers

Strategic KPIs are as follows:

- **Direct traffic, number of all visitors, whether online or in stores**: These are the result of certain company activity. We will only measure the number of identified or unique visitors.
- **Indirect traffic, number of all visitors, whether online or in stores**: These are not the result of certain company activity. We will only measure the number of identified or unique visitors.
- **Unidentified traffic source**: We will measure all traffic for which we cannot identify the source.
- **Brand recognition**: The number of brand mentions in all possible media outlets.
- **Conversion rate**: The percentage of interactions that were converted into sales.
- **Rate of adoption**: The number of customers that have adopted a product or service, divided by the total number of unique interactions.
- **Average order value by channel**: Total sales revenue per channel, divided by the number of transactions.

Retention (monetize relationship)

For companies, it is paramount to reduce churn and increase the value of customers. When talking about retention, these are the important points to consider:

- The company needs to create loyalty, and doing so prevent customers using the services or products of another company.
- The company needs to create brand ambassadors out of customers. This process is critical in this era of increased social influence and word-of-mouth.
- Raise the value of customers, as the company needs to be able to increase value based on basis of its current customers by using up-sell or cross-sell offerings.

Retention KPIs

We will group KPIs into two groups, strategic and operational. KPIs will enable us to measure the progress of retention efforts.

Operational KPIs are as follows:

- **Sentiment**: Written text sentiment that is measured on social media using specialized tools
- **Average resolution time**: Average time needed for case resolution, grouped by case type
- **Uptime**: Percentage of time per year that service has been available
- **Cost of the channel**: Total costs associated with each channel

Strategic KPIs are as follows:

- **Churn rate**: Number of all customers that fail to make a purchase in a defined amount of time or that cancel the service
- **Net promoter score**: Scale from 0-10 identifying how customers are influencing the brand's promotion
- **Customer satisfaction**: Percentage of customers that are satisfied with the customer experience
- **Effort**: The effort that customer needs to invest to go through the interaction with the company

Efficiency (leverage investment)

Operational excellence is the cornerstone of every efficient company. Efficiency means that the company is able to achieve greater earnings while lowering costs.

The main topics to be considered regarding efficiency are as follows:

- The company needs to be able to increase **Return on Investment** (**ROI**). Increase in ROI usually means that the company is performing better.
- The company needs to be able to lower its operational costs. Lowering operational costs without impacting the quality of its CX means that the company will earn more.
- The company must be able to increase productivity. Increased productivity can be quantified as the impact that each employee has on delivering the best possible customer experience.

Efficiency KPIs

We will group KPIs into two groups, strategic and operational. KPIs will enable us to measure the progress of efficiency efforts.

Operational KPIs are as follows:

- **First contact resolution**: Percentage of cases resolved in one interaction
- **Average handle time**: Average time needed per interaction with customer
- **Retention cost per customer**: Cost of retention initiatives divided by number of participating customers
- **Escalation percentage**: Percentage of interactions that have been escalated
- **Training time**: Total number of hours needed for a new employees to start working independently

Strategic KPIs are as follows:

- **Sales cost**: All costs associated with selling of products or services
- **Marketing costs**: All costs associated with marketing and promotion activities
- **Service costs**: All costs associated with customers product or service use
- **Activity costs**: Per channel, the total cost divided by the number of interactions
- **Automated service rate**: Percentage of interactions that have been completed by customers without employee interactions

It is of utmost importance that KPIs and associated values are adjusted according to the company's mission and objectives because KPIs will be the main tool used in measuring the success of CX implementation.

Summary

The velocity of technological advancement and the velocity of customer adoption of these technologies has led to consistent and large changes in customer behavior and expectations. This has led to a shift in influence from companies to customers.

Today's business environment is becoming more and more competitive each day, so companies are beginning to grasp that customer experience is of strategical value, and not just nice to have.

To be successful in today's business environment, companies must realize the following:

- A customer experience that consists of multiple channels that contribute to the relationship with customer
- A customer experience that is affected by every part of the company

Only a holistic approach spanning all systems and departments of the company can enable appropriate customer experience. The main objectives that need to be addressed are as follows:

- Seamless cross-channel experience
- Consistent experience
- Faster time to market
- Operational excellence

Only by having excellent customer experience will a company be able to acquire new customers, retain existing customers, and reduce operational costs.

I hope this last chapter and the book as a whole will help you to try out the Oracle CX Suite and explore its various products.

Other Books You May Enjoy

If you enjoyed this book, you may be interested in these other books by Packt:

Implementing Oracle API Platform Cloud Service
Andrew Bell, Sander Rensen, Luis Weir, Phil Wilkins

ISBN: 9781788478656

- Get an overview of the Oracle API Cloud Service Platform
- See typical use cases of the Oracle API Cloud Service Platform
- Design your own APIs using Apiary
- Build and run microservices
- Set up API gateways with the new API platform from Oracle
- Customize developer portals
- Configuration management
- Implement Oauth 2.0 policies
- Implement custom policies
- Get a policy SDK overview
- Transition from Oracle API Management 12c to the new Oracle API platform

Blockchain across Oracle
Robert van Mölken

ISBN: 9781788474290

- A full introduction to the Blockchain
- How the Blockchain affects Oracle developers and customers
- Core concepts including blocks, hashes, and chains, assets, transactions, and consensus
- How to work with Oracle Cloud to implement a Blockchain Network
- Design, develop, and run smart contracts on the Oracle Blockchain Cloud Service
- Blockchain security and privacy for Oracle developers and clients
- Public and private Blockchain decisions for Oracle architects and developers
- Industry analysis across finance, governance, and healthcare sectors
- Industry trends and the future of the Blockchain technology

Leave a review - let other readers know what you think

Please share your thoughts on this book with others by leaving a review on the site that you bought it from. If you purchased the book from Amazon, please leave us an honest review on this book's Amazon page. This is vital so that other potential readers can see and use your unbiased opinion to make purchasing decisions, we can understand what our customers think about our products, and our authors can see your feedback on the title that they have worked with Packt to create. It will only take a few minutes of your time, but is valuable to other potential customers, our authors, and Packt. Thank you!

Index

www.ingramcontent.com/pod-product-compliance
Lightning Source LLC
Chambersburg PA
CBHW080636060326
40690CB00021B/4954